# Knox County 2012 Charter Review Committee

# Knox County 2012 Charter Review Committee

PERSONAL NOTES AND POSITION PAPERS

David L. Page, Ph.D.

Warped Minds Press

Knoxville, Tennessee

Copyright © 2024 by David L. Page, Ph.D.

All rights reserved. No part of this publication may be reproduced, distributed, or transmitted in any form or by any means, including photocopying, recording, or other electronic or mechanical methods, without the prior written permission of the publisher, except in the case of brief quotations embodied in critical reviews and certain other noncommercial uses permitted by copyright law. For permission requests, write to the publisher, addressed "Attention: Permissions Coordinator," at the address below.

Warped Minds Press
8410 Corteland Drive
Knoxville, Tennessee 37909
www.warpedminds.io

Book Layout ©2017 BookDesignTemplates.com

Ordering Information:

Quantity sales. Special discounts are available on quantity purchases by corporations, associations, and others. Contact the "Special Sales Department" at the address above for details.

Knox County 2012 Charter Review Committee/David L. Page. Ph.D.—1st ed.

ISBN 979-8-9906504-3-5 (Paperback)
ISBN 979-8-9906504-4-2 (eBook)

*For my late mother, Shirley, and my late father, Bob, who taught me through their example the responsibility of being an engaged citizen.*

*All politics is local.*

—Tip O'Neill

# Contents

The Committee ............................................................. 1
    Charter Review Committee
    First Meetings

Meeting: March 28 ..................................................... 5
    Uniformed Officers Pension Plan
    Two-Thirds (2/3) Vote

Meeting: May 23 ....................................................... 13
    Term Definition
    Uniformed Officers Pension Plan (Again)
    Ballot Size
    Further Discussion

Meeting: June 27 ..................................................... 33
    Appoint or Elect (Bureaucrats vs. Politicians)
    Fee Offices

Conclusions ............................................................. 59

Acknowledgments .................................................. 61

Appendix ................................................................. 65
    Forms of Local Government
    Common Questions for Appoint-Elect Debate
    Common Questions for Salary Suit Debate
    Proposed Amendments to Article IX of the Charter
    Knox County Charter

Work Cited ............................................................ 139

INTRODUCTION

# The Committee

ON JANUARY 23, 2012, the Knox County Commission in Tennessee met and appointed members to serve on the Knox County Charter Review commission. Knox County has a form of government known as "Home Rule," which differs from other counties throughout Tennessee. The State of Tennessee dictates the form of government for 93 of the 95 counties in Tennessee, but for Knox County and Shelby County, the citizens have chosen to specify their form of government through a charter. Such a charter form of county government is authorized under the State Constitution. By adopting a charter, the voters in Knox and Shelby are authorized to approve specific changes to the structure and governance of their counties. For example, both counties have a provision for term limits on county offices.

The Knox County Charter also includes a provision for periodic review of the charter to ensure the government functions appropriately. To this end, the Knox County Charter requires that a Charter Review Committee be constituted every eight years to determine the desirability of amendments to the Charter. This committee is the one that I served on, and it led to the generation of the personal notes and position papers found in this bound volume. The appointed members of the committee for 2012 appear on the following page. I was nominated by the Sixth District Commission Brad Anders and then appointed to the committee by the vote of the full Knox County Commission.

## Charter Review Committee

Appointed: January 23, 2012 (Update: March 2012)
Total of 27 members:

> 9 Mayoral appointments, approved by the Commission;
> 9 Citizens appointed by the Commission for each district;
> 9 Commissioner, one for each district.

### *Mayoral Appointment, Approved by Commission (9)*

> Teressa Williams
> John Schmid
> Phyllis Nichols
> Billy Stokes
> Diane Jablonski
> Tony Parker
> Beth Wade
> Lisa Starbuck
> Brad Suneson

### *Commission Appointments (9)*

> Keith Lindsey
> Renee Hoyos
> Randall Smith

Personal Notes and Position Papers

Barbara Pelot
Craig Leuthold
David Page
Bob Rountree
Ann Acuff
Ed Frahme

*Commissioners (9)*

Sam McKenzie
Amy Broyles
Tony Norman
Jeff Ownby
Richard Briggs
Brad Anders
R. Larry Smith
Dave Wright
Mike Brown

The official list includes the names, corresponding phone numbers, and residential addresses. I have omitted the latter as such information is no longer relevant and, in some cases, valid. I remember receiving a call from my Commissioner, Brad Anders, asking if I would be willing and available to serve. I was excited about the opportunity, and at the time, I was a small business owner in our three-company startup, Third Dimension Technologies. I remember taking the call at my desk in our incubator space—the things we remember.

## First Meetings

The Committee's first official meeting was on February 5, 2012, in the Main Assembly Room of the City-County

Building at 400 Main Street in Knoxville. Knox County Law Director Joseph Jarret conducted this meeting. He gave an overview presentation of the Knox County Charter and the committee's charge. He made it clear that the committee would need to appoint a chair.

We subsequently met again on February 15 and 29, selected Craig Leuthold as the chair, and agreed on the rules. As far as I remember, these first few meetings were brief and non-substantive. We struggled to gain our footing regarding the committee's mission. That said, I anticipated that topics of importance would arise at the next meeting on March 28. Unfortunately, I would not be able to make the meeting.

As a result, I drafted my thoughts and opinions and sent them to Chairperson Leuthold. I developed personal notes and position papers expressing my views and presenting information for discussion. I did not necessarily intend for these notes and papers to be conclusive opinions. Instead, I intended them to spawn and encourage public debate. The following chapters are the meetings and the topics on the agenda for those meetings. I did not have access to the agenda, which would have been helpful to recollect the sequence of topics. I have attempted to organize the dates from my files. I have made minor edits, but the content follows the notes and papers written in 2012.

CHAPTER 1

# Meeting: March 28

THE MARCH 28, 2012, MEETING of the Charter Review Committee is when I first began to draft position papers and personal notes. I had a prior commitment with my business that I could not reschedule, and thus, I could not attend. During that meeting, I anticipated the committee may discuss two topics of importance, and I wanted to make sure my input was put before the committee.

As a result, I wrote the following letter to the committee chair and included two position papers I drafted to discuss my points of interest.

David L. Page
5707 Copperleaf Drive
Knoxville, TN 37931

March 22, 2012

Craig Leuthold
Chairman
Knox County Charter Review Committee
400 West Main Street, Suite 603
Knoxville, TN 37902

Dear Chairman Leuthold,

I am writing to you as I cannot attend the March 28th meeting of the Knox County Charter Review Committee. I have a prior business commitment and will not be in Tennessee.

With this letter, I wanted to pass along to you and the other Committee members a few thoughts regarding items on the Committee agenda for that meeting. Please find the attached White Papers with this letter that hopefully express my views on the following:

1. The Uniformed Officers Pension Plan
2. The Two-Thirds Vote Language

This letter and associated White Papers are available for public release in whatever form the Office of the Law Director deems appropriate. I have copied him on this letter.

Sincerely,

// Signed

David L. Page
Sixth District Commission Appointee
Knox County Charter Review Committee

CC: Joe Jarrett (Law Director), Members of Charter Review Committee

Figure 1. Letter to Craig Leuthold on March 22, 2012.

Personal Notes and Position Papers

# Uniformed Officers Pension Plan

The following text represents the content of the position paper for the argument to the Charter Review Committee.

## Delay Discussion

The Committee has discussed the pros and cons of considering the Uniformed Officers Pension Plan (UOPP). In keeping with the Committee's desire to methodically step through the Charter and address issues in the order they appear, I would argue that we should delay discussing the UOPP until we reach Article VII.

## Advantages

The advantage of delaying UOPP discussion is twofold.

First, the County Commission wants to address the UOPP independently. A delay by the Charter Review Committee would give the Commission time to take action and express its views. The Commission may create its own ballot initiative or forward its views to this Committee. Either way, this Committee can review the Commission's actions and act as we see fit.

Second, the delay will give this Committee time to "come up to speed" on the UOPP issues. I would suggest that this Committee seek written explanations from the parties involved (Office of the Sheriff, Pension Board, Office of the Mayor, etc.) Such descriptions should be as brief as possible and focus strictly on what Charter amendments (if any) are recommended to address the UOPP challenges. My desire for written explanations is to seek concise and thoughtful language from the parties involved. To this end, I would recommend something along the lines of a three-page limit. (Note that the discussion of the UOPP in the Charter is essentially a single page.)

## Knox County Voters

My personal view is that the UOPP is an important benefit that is necessary for the Sheriff to recruit and maintain highly qualified officers. Eliminating the UOPP seems ill-advised since the voters of Knox County, by passing the original UOPP amendment, would appear to agree to the need for the UOPP. This Committee should consider the weight of this prior vote by Knox County citizens.

## Pension Board Handcuffs

The current financial (and political) challenge facing the UOPP is the limited power of the Pension Board, as outlined in the Charter, to sustain a financially viable UOPP without austere County budgets. As I read the language in Sec. 7.05, the Charter has essentially handcuffed the Pension Board into unsustainable commitments, given the current economic realities.

## Check and Balance

The Charter established the Pension Board as a political check and balance to "adopt and administer a financially sound retirement system." Thus, the solutions to the UOPP challenges seem simple. However, I confess that I may not be financially smart or politically savvy enough to understand the complexities reported and purported about the UOPP fully.

Amendment of the UOPP is necessary to maintain the spirit of the UOPP while strengthening the check and balance oversight of the Pension Board. I would argue for consideration of the following avenues.

First, amend the UOPP language to give the Pension Board more flexibility to change UOPP terms (vesting, % salary, COLA, etc.). Such amendments should maintain the spirit of the UOPP while also providing the Pension Board with sufficient leeway and margins to meet their financial soundness charge. I would discourage stringent definitions of the UOPP terms, as the Charter currently does, to avoid the handcuff problem that Knox County now faces. The amendment language should provide the Pension Board with broad guidelines (rather than detailed terms) for the UOPP. The Pension Board comprises elected officials and pension stakeholders and is thus suitably equipped to adjust UOPP terms as economic situations warrant.

Second, the UOPP should be recognized as a special pension within Knox County's Charter. The Sheriff of Knox County should be an ex officio member of the Pension Board. The inclusion of the Sheriff on the Pension Board has some drawbacks, particularly concerning fairness to other elected offices. However, those drawbacks are outweighed by the need for the Office of the Sheriff to maintain a suitable UOPP for the officers and deputies of Knox County.

*Summary*

I urge the Charter Review Committee to consider delaying addressing the UOPP until it reaches Article VII. I would then urge that the Committee weigh the prior votes of Knox County citizens in favor of the UOPP. Finally, I would argue for a Charter amendment that maintains the spirit and intent of the UOPP while strengthening the Pension Board's check-and-balance role.

## Two-Thirds (2/3) Vote

The second item I anticipated the committee to review is the following text, which argues for strictly rounding up in non-integer ratio calculations of votes. During the earlier meetings, a side discussion occurred, during which committee members were confused about this issue and offered opinions on "what the Constitution" said. I found these arguments unsatisfying and wanted to ensure we followed good practice. This position paper is a result of that effort.

### Argument for Strictly Rounding Up

At the March 14 meeting of the Charter Review Committee, members discussed the definition of two-thirds voting in the Knox County Charter (e.g., Sec. 2.02.H "affirmative vote of two-thirds (2/3) of the entire Commission") and the need for clarity in the Charter. Some Committee members suggested using the "round half up" convention as a definition. I would argue against this convention and instead argue for a more robust (and more legally defensible) "strictly round up" approach.

### Strictly Round-Up

As I read the Charter, the sections with two-thirds language indicated that two-thirds is a threshold. As a threshold, the affirmative vote count must equal or exceed two-thirds, which means that at least two-thirds of affirmative votes are necessary. Thus, for an 11-member Commission, eight (8) or more affirmative votes satisfy the two-thirds threshold, while seven (7) or fewer votes do not. This rounding convention is strictly a round-up convention.

## Round Half Up

During the meeting, the "round half-up" convention was discussed. This convention is probably the one folks are most familiar with, as it is commonly taught in school. Using this convention, one would arrive at seven (7) affirmative votes for an 11-member Commission since two-thirds of 11 is 7.333. With the round half-up convention, this value rounds down to seven. However, seven is less than two-thirds and does not satisfy the two-thirds threshold. Simply put, 7/11 does meet or not exceed 2/3.

## Precedent

The interpretation of the US Constitution and Robert's Rules of Order also promote the strict round-up convention for fractional votes. While definitions from these sources do not necessarily bind Knox County, their authority offers a strong precedent that is difficult to ignore.

## Summary

If this Committee desires to clarify the two-thirds language in the Charter, I would urge the adoption of the strictly round-up definition as outlined here rather than the weaker definition of round-half-up (or other equally weak conventions).

CHAPTER 2

# Meeting: May 23

THE APRIL 25 MEETING was uneventful as I recall. I wish I had kept the meeting minutes. With the May 23 meeting, I was gaining momentum in my research and writing about the topics of interest. By way of introduction, I again wrote the following letter to the Chair and included two position papers that I drafted to discuss my points of interest. I again revisited the UOPP.

David L. Page
5707 Copperleaf Drive
Knoxville, TN 37931

May 6, 2012

Craig Leuthold
Chairman
Knox County Charter Review Committee
400 West Main Street, Suite 603
Knoxville, TN 37902

Dear Chairman Leuthold,

With this letter, I wanted to pass along a few thoughts to you and the other Committee members regarding items on the agenda for the May 9, 2012, meeting. Please find the attached White Papers with this letter that hopefully express my views on the following:

    1. Term Limits and Definition of a Term
    2. The Uniformed Officers Pension Plan

Thank you, and I look forward to discussing these topics.

Sincerely,

  // Signed

David L. Page
Sixth District Commission Appointee
Knox County Charter Review Committee

CC: Joe Jarrett (Law Director), Members of Charter Review Committee

Figure 2. Letter to Craig Leuthold on May 6, 2012.

# Term Definition

Term Limits were a controversial issue that sparked significant debate. Within that debate is the issue of what constitutes a full term or, alternatively, a partial term. Below, I present an argument in support of what was known as "Option 2" or "The Acuff Proposal."

## Argument for Acuff (Option 2) Proposal

An item before the Charter Review Committee is defining a term concerning term limits (E. R. Board, 2012; Bonavita, 2012). For Knox County offices (Mayor, Commissioners, etc.), a full term is typically four years (for simplicity, the one-time six-year commission terms are ignored in this white paper). Exceptions occur when a special election or appointment fills an office.

**Special Election**

Since Knox County holds elections on a two-year cycle, a special or regular election for any office will occur within two years of an office vacancy. So, a special election would result in a person holding office for a two-year term rather than a four-year term.

**Appointment**

Because of the two-year election cycle, no appointed person would hold an office for over two years (plus some margin for election organization). Thus, an appointed official would face a special or regular election within two years.

## Proposed Amendments

This Committee is currently considering two proposals.

**Schmid (Option 1) Proposal**

Committee member John Schmid has put forward an amendment to align the definition of a term with the 22nd Amendment of the US Constitution ("U.S. Const., amend. XXII,")The spirit of the Schmid proposal is to allow a maximum of 10 years in a particular office. As a result, this proposal would also lead to situations where an officeholder might serve just six (6) years due to a special election counting as a full term.

- Max possible time: slightly more than ten years
- Min possible time: slightly more than six years

**Acuff (Option 2) Proposal**

Committee member Ann Acuff has proposed an alternative amendment to define a full term as four years. Anything less would be a partial (incomplete) term. Thus, time in office by appointment or special election would not count against a person's term-limit clock.

- Max possible time: Less than 12 years
- Min possible time: Exactly eight years (two full terms)

*A Slice of Pizza Does Not a Pizza Make*

I am strongly for the Acuff (Option 2) proposal. Appointments and special elections lead to partial terms and should not be counted against the term-limit clock. A partial term is not a full term, just as a slice of pizza is not a pizza. It's something less than a pizza—it's a slice.

**Loopholes of 22nd Amendment Analogy**

At first glance, the Schmid Proposal to align the Knox County Charter with the 22nd Amendment looks pretty comforting. As a patriotic American, that response is natural. The US

Constitution is an amazing document and should not be casually dismissed. However, as one digs deeper, the fallacy of this analogy becomes apparent, and that comforting feeling is simply an emotional—rather than logical—response to our Constitution's heritage.

*Apples to Oranges*

The office of the US President and the elected offices of Knox County are very different in scope and power. Comparing them is like comparing apples to oranges.

The 22nd Amendment applies only to the President and no other federal office. The US Constitution establishes a robust executive branch embodied in the President. By contrast, the Knox County Charter establishes a strong legislative branch embodied in the Commission. These models are quite different forms of government (*County Leadership Handbook 2008: Special Edition, National Association of Counties, Revised March 2011.*).

The strong executive model (Constitution) and strong legislative model (Charter) are diametrically opposed. The 22nd Amendment is a formal limitation of the robust executive model and has little (if any) parallel to the strong legislative model of Knox County. The exclusion of other offices in the 22nd Amendment is very noteworthy and should be weighed when considering the Schmid Proposal.

The US President has enormous power and is rightly limited to a minimum of six (6) years and a maximum of 10 years. No elected office in Knox County has nearly the level or magnitude of power as the President, and thus, the Acuff Proposal is more reasonable.

While few would turn down being President even for a day, Knox County has to look no further than the Law Director's office to see that one might turn down even a six-month appointment. The Acuff Proposal is essential to guarantee that the most qualified for office are willing to serve and that the will of the people is carried out.

## Clear Line of Succession

The US Presidency has a clear line of succession (Neale, 2009). As such, special elections and appointments do not occur for this office. Individuals (Vice President, Speaker of the House, etc.) that might serve a partial term in the Presidency know well beforehand that they may be called upon.

This knowledge and the federal succession infrastructure reduce the learning curve for a partial-term President. Thus, the shorter service times imposed by the 22nd Amendment are justifiable. An appointed President is prepared to quickly come up to speed to execute the duties and responsibilities of her office effectively.

With Knox County elected offices, special elections and appointments stretch out the learning curve for these offices since no line of succession is known a priori and no infrastructure exists to support succession. Special elections and appointments thrust an individual into office with little preparation time. Thus, the longer service times of the Acuff Proposal are more appropriate.

**Balance of Knowledge and Power**

The core difference between the Acuff and Schmid Proposals is balancing effectiveness through institutional knowledge versus the opportunity for institutional abuse. Schmid attempts to curb institutional abuse by reducing time in office and, thus, time in power. On the other hand, Acuff attempts to leverage the benefits of institutional knowledge that comes with time in office.

With a strong legislative model of government, the executive branch is often spread over several different elected offices (Sanford et al., 2012). As with Knox County, the executive is spread through elected row offices: the Mayor, the Trustee, the Register of Deeds, the Sheriff, etc. The institutional knowledge gained from time in office is quite valuable.

Therefore, the Acuff proposal is important because it allows Knox County to reap the benefits of this knowledge when voters desire to give an additional term to an elected official.

Term limits are the balance to keep institutional knowledge from morphing into institutional abuse. The power of the office is undoubtedly seductive, but with Knox County's strong legislative model, no office holds sufficient power to justify imposing strong term limit constraints relative to the Schmid proposal.

The Acuff proposal recognizes the benefits of institutional knowledge while striking a proper balance with time in office and term limits.

**A Long-Term View**

The argument for term limits is easy to grasp. "Power tends to corrupt, and absolute power corrupts absolutely." The consensus among voters is to throw the dirty scoundrels out of office. The challenge before this Committee is to not overreact to this sentiment and to take a more long-term view of what is best for the county.

The Schmid Proposal is—though well-intentioned—a potential overreaction. Research suggests that term limits have only modest effects, if any, on public policy at the local level (McGlynn & Sylvester, 2010), with some studies suggesting unintended negative effects (Alexandar, 2011; Chen, 2008).

The objective of this committee is to present to the voters amendments that consider the county's long-term interests and are not simply knee-jerk reactions to populist sentiments. The popularity of term limits among voters is undeniable, and this committee should carefully balance that popularity with good policy.

The Acuff Proposal takes a longer view. Specifically, individuals considering whether or not to accept an appointment to office should not have to go through the political calculus of term-limit clocks. The Schmid Proposal would induce such calculations in future appointments, whereas the Acuff Proposal would not.

The Acuff Proposal errors on the side of quality appointments over political considerations.

## Conclusion

I urge this Committee to adopt the Acuff (Option 2) Proposal, which strikes a proper balance of institutional knowledge and takes a longer view of county interests.

# Uniformed Officers Pension Plan (Again)

The UOPP was again on the agenda, and I prepared a more extended position paper for this meeting, which I wrote on May 9, 2012. The following text outlines the argument for supporting the UOPP.

## Support of Defined Benefit Plans for Officers

The Charter Review Committee is considering an amendment to close the current Uniformed Officers Pension Plan (UOPP) and to mandate the pension board to create a new, enhanced UOPP to replace it (Bonavita, 2012).

## The Positives of Defined Benefit Plans

While I have not decided whether or not to support the proposed amendment as written on the May 9 Agenda (Bonavita, 2012), it is important to clear the air about the role of a defined benefit plan in the Sheriff's Department.

To be clear, there is nothing evil about a defined benefit plan. The county's financial woes are not the result of a defined benefit plan but rather of its implementation. Defined benefit plans—though not common in the private sector—are pretty common in the public sector, particularly for law enforcement (Munnell et al., 2007).

**Government Is Not a Business: The Thin Blue Line**
Chris Caldwell, Knox County's Accounting and Budgeting Manager, came before this Committee and asked a question (perhaps rhetorically) regarding what businesses contribute at the levels Knox County does on behalf of their employees towards defined benefit plans.

Not to grandstand too much, but the question that I would ask (perhaps rhetorically) is what businesses ask men and women to stand on the Thin Blue Line between chaos and order, law and lawlessness, badges and bullets, and life and death. Government—particularly law enforcement—is not a profit-motivated business. May God have mercy on our souls on the day they become one.

Mr. Caldwell's misguided question is that he has perhaps lost sight of the role of the Sheriff's department and, thus, the defined benefit plan that serves that department. Examples abound for defined benefit plans with significant employer contributions towards those plans in government.

Perhaps the best-known is the US military, which rewards 20 years of service at half salary. Uncle Sam contributes 100% to this plan with zero "employee" contribution. Likewise, the FBI, almost every federal law enforcement agency, and many state and local public safety agencies throughout the US have defined benefit plans (*Detailed Review of Retirement Plan Trends, Best Practices, and Innovations by Other Public and Private-Sector Employers*, 2008; Munnell et al., 2007).

## A Young Man's Game Requiring Seasoned Wisdom

One of the main reasons the US military and law enforcement agencies opt for defined benefit plans is the need to attract young individuals who are athletically suitable for the rigors of the job while retaining seasoned veterans with hard-earned wisdom about the local beats they protect.

Defined benefit plans are essential to maintain this balance of a wise yet youthful force. When a young man or woman decides to join a law enforcement agency, that choice is not just for a nine-to-five job but a calling (Caudill & Peak, 2009). Thus, law enforcement is not a stepping stone to some other career; the choice pigeonholes individuals as they undergo a protracted training period.

Law enforcement officers' skills are invaluable to the public good but are difficult to translate to private sector jobs. Defined benefit plans help ensure that officers stay with an agency so that the public reaps the benefits of their in-depth training and on-the-job knowledge.

At the other end of the spectrum, an officer working past his prime regarding physical and mental readiness is a problem an agency would hope to avoid. A defined benefit plan is critical to ensuring officers decide to retire based on job readiness and not financial readiness (Caudill & Peak, 2009).

As a side note, the News Sentinel has rightly pointed out that this debate is not about officers' mortality rates (Donila, 2011d). However, the stressors that law enforcement officers face are quite different from those found in their civilian counterparts.

**Retaining Officers—Anecdotal Evidence**

While I have no evidence other than anecdotes, retaining well-trained officers is another critical component of the need for a defined benefit plan such as the UOPP. Through personal conversations, I am aware of a few former officers trained either by the Knox County Sheriff's Office or by the Knoxville City Police Department who have leveraged their training to seek "greener" pastures in federal law enforcement or federal security contractors.

Better pay and benefits have been the primary reasons for using these local law enforcement agencies as stepping stones. I understand such anecdotes are weak evidence, but they are nonetheless evidence.

Retaining officers is an essential factor in the UOPP.

## Conclusion: Begrudging the Badge

Like most folks, my 401k plan has been cut in half by the economic downturns over the past few years to become a 201k plan. Most of us have defined contribution plans, and it's easy to begrudge Knox County deputies and the UOPP.

We should resist this urge.

Sheriff's deputies' role in our government is at the foundation of our American government—establishing justice and ensuring domestic tranquility for us, the people ("U.S. Const., pmbl.,"). The Sheriff's department and the deputies who serve us should be high on the list of where our local tax dollars should go. Though the UOPP plan needs reform, we should not throw the baby out with the bath water.

## Ballot Size

The final position paper for this chapter concerns ballot fatigue. The Charter Review Committee will present the results of our work to Knox County citizens for a vote. Will ballot fatigue be an issue?

### Argument for Due Diligence

The Charter Review Committee faces the challenge of placing many Charter amendments on upcoming August and November (2012) ballots. The concern is that the anticipated volume of such amendments and the resulting ballot size may lead to ballot fatigue (Burnham, 1965) and overwhelm Knox County voters.

### Positions

During previous meetings, two distinguished committee members have put forward two different positions on ballot size.

**Ms. Broyles' Position**

Commissioner Amy Broyles has argued that this Committee should limit the scope of its work and focus on significant amendments, thereby maintaining a smaller ballot.

**Ms. Jablonski's Position**

Committee member Diane Jablonski has argued that this Committee should maintain a broad scope and conduct due diligence regardless of the final ballot size.

## Personal Notes and Position Papers

### *Shirking Our Responsibility*

While remaining sympathetic to Ms. Broyles' position, the Charter Review Committee should be careful not to shirk our responsibility if we do not follow Ms. Jablonski's position. Knox County voters deserve our best effort, regardless of the ballot size. Proper due diligence should be our guide rather than paternalism for voters.

We do not have a crystal ball to discern the complexities of ballot psychology, and we should spend little time on such exercises. Our job is clear: We are to put before voters amendments that improve Knox County and the Charter that governs us.

That said, the Committee should consider the research and evidence regarding "ballot fatigue," and we should work responsibly to mitigate such issues. The following discussion advances this due diligence position while offering avenues for reducing ballot fatigue.

### *"Voters Are Not Fools," Resisting Paternalism*

Academic research on ballot fatigue is plentiful, and a popular thesis among political academics is that American voters are not very sophisticated (Campbell et al., 1960). This disconnected view from ivory towers portrays little confidence in the average voter—a dangerous proposition. To which the academic V. O. Key famously replied, "Voters are not fools" (Key, 1966).

We should carefully heed Key's advice (and research) in digesting the literature and view ballot fatigue with some skepticism. Key and others (Gershkoff, 2005; Popkin, 1991) have demonstrated that while the average voter may not become the next Jeopardy champion, their collective wisdom (Surowiecki, 2005) ensures the continued success of democracy.

In light of Key, Knox County voters are more than capable of sifting the wheat from the chaff to sort out Charter amendments both big and small. We should resist the urge to drift toward paternalism (Mill, 1989) by limiting the number of amendments on the ballot for the "good" of the voter. They are not fools, and we should not treat them as such.

## *Ballot Fatigue*

However, this committee would be remiss in our duty to voters if we did not consider the effects of ballot fatigue and plan to mitigate any negative consequences.

Looking at the research (Augenblick & Nicholson, 2016; Bullock III & Dunn, 1996; Burnham, 1965; Dubin & Kalsow, 1996, 1997; Kimball & Kropf, 2008; Mueller, 1969; Reilly & Richey, 2011; Reilly et al., 2012; Wattenberg et al., 2000), ballot fatigue is the process whereby voters vote for the top-of-the-ballot contests but do not vote on bottom-of-the-ballot ones. The problem is well known and is often called "roll-off," whereby votes roll off on down-ballot issues. In simpler terms, some voters do not complete their ballots.

A variety of variables influence ballot fatigue (or roll-off), with most researchers agreeing on three general areas: (a) lack of voter interest,(b) barriers with voting technology, and (c) variations in voter demographics (e.g., socio-economics, education, etc.) (Bullock III & Dunn, 1996; Kimball & Kropf, 2008).

With Knox County voting machines, item (b) is particularly interesting as we have a rotating dial to advance down a particular ballot page. This dial induces a minor barrier like an antiquated rotary phone is a hassle to dial. We can all agree that rotating that blasted dial can lead to ballot fatigue in Knox County.

While ballot fatigue seems intuitively negative, other researchers (Augenblick & Nicholson, 2016; Dubin & Kalsow, 1997; Gordon, 2011; Tolbert et al., 2001) have identified positive effects from long ballots. In particular, ballots with an elevated number of initiatives typically yield higher voter turnouts (Gordon, 2011; Tolbert et al., 2001). The theory is that more issues on the ballot lead to more media coverage, heightening voter engagement.

Additionally, some researchers (Augenblick & Nicholson, 2016; Dubin & Kalsow, 1997) suggest that votes on down-ballot issues come from more informed voters who better understand the issues. As one political blogger noted, "This ballot will be a challenge for the average voter [but] for the political junkie, it will be heaven on earth" (Buffer, 2011).

To Ms. Broyles' position, the research noted above would indicate that ballot fatigue could play a part in the amendment outcomes, but as the next section suggests, remedies are possible to minimize the effect.

## *Suggested Remedies*

The above research suggests some common-sense remedies that the Committee can leverage to minimize ballot fatigue.

**Easy to read ballot.**

A major factor in roll-off is the readability of ballot questions (Reilly & Richey, 2011). Questions often use "lawyer speak" and legalistic language that is difficult to comprehend. The US Department of Education (Kirsch, 1994) recommends framing questions at an eighth-grade reading level to ensure accessibility by the average American. This Committee should adopt this standard and insist on readable language for ballot questions. Readability and grade-level equivalent are readily computed using standard tools in Microsoft Word (the Flesch Score and the Flesch-Kincaid Grade Score).

**Specify ballot order.**
Clearly, down-ballot issues receive less attention from voters. As I understand the Election Commission's process (Mackay, 2012), this Committee dictates the order in which questions appear on the amendment section of the ballot. Subsequently, we should prioritize ballot questions so that the most important amendments appear first, thereby ensuring that the most salient issues appear before potential voter roll-off.

**Consistency and affirmative voting.**
To reduce confusion, each amendment question should have a similar construction to afford consistency across the ballot. The question should be framed such that a "yes" vote means to amend the Charter while a "no" vote means to maintain the status quo (Olsen, 2006). The ballot should not toggle between constructions such that "yes" changes the Charter on one question while "no" changes the Charter on another question. The following question is a possible template:

> "Shall Section_____ of the Knox County Charter be amended to provide_____?"

**Distribute questions over multiple election ballots.**
The Committee has discussed this remedy extensively with general consensus regarding placing amendment questions on the August and November 2012 election ballots. The current operating principle is to put less controversial amendments on the August ballot, with more important amendments appearing on the December ballot. A third option, not yet considered, is for this Committee to remain seated past the November 2012 election (if just for one day past) and to defer

some amendment questions to the 2014 election cycle. One thought is to defer minor and less controversial amendments to 2014, thereby reducing the number of questions on the 2012 ballots.

**Education about proposed amendments.**

My sense is that this Committee is very aware of our responsibility to educate voters about proposed amendments. Research suggests that "getting the word out" is invaluable in increasing voter turnout and reducing ballot roll-off. I only list this remedy for completeness.

*Summary*

In summary, the Committee should consider ballot fatigue within the sobering context of paternalism. Following Ms. Jablonski's position, we have a duty of due diligence to Knox County voters. Although ballot fatigue is a concern, the above-proposed remedies offer common sense and reasonable approaches to mitigate roll-off issues.

**Status of Possible Amendments**

The following table summarizes the status of amendments under consideration by the Committee as of the May 9, 2012, meeting.

David L. Page, Ph.D.

Table 1. Amendment Status on May 9, 2012.

|  | Amendment | On List | On 1st Read | Pass 1st | Pass 2nd |
|---|---|---|---|---|---|
| 1 | Sec. 1.02. Private & local affairs |  |  |  | Yes |
| 2 | Sec. 2.02.I Other Powers |  |  |  | Yes |
| 3 | Sec. 2.02.A Other Powers |  |  |  | Yes |
| 4 | Sec. 2.03.C Membership & election |  |  |  | Yes |
| 5 | Sec. 6.01.E Board of Education |  |  |  | Yes |
| 6 | Sec. 9.03.I Definitions |  |  |  | Yes |
| 7 | Sec. 2.02.B Other Powers |  |  | Yes |  |
| 8 | Sec. 2.09.B Ordinances |  |  | Yes |  |
| 9 | Sec. 9.17.A Term Limits |  |  | Yes |  |
| 10 | Sec. 6.01.B Board of Education |  | Yes |  |  |
| 11 | Sec. 7.05 UOPP |  | Yes |  |  |
| 12 | Sec. 8.01, 8.02 Elections |  | Yes |  |  |
| 13 | Sec. 3.08, 4.01-05 Appt. Row Offices | Yes |  |  |  |
| 14 | Sec. 3.08, 4.01-05 Charter Offices | Yes |  |  |  |
| 15 | Sec. 3.07 Budget Procedures | Yes |  |  |  |
| 16 | Sec. 7.03 Size of Pension Board | Yes |  |  |  |
| 17 | Sec. 3.08 Law Director Qualifications | Yes |  |  |  |
| 18 | Sec. 2.03 Commission Size | No |  |  |  |

## Further Discussion

In addition to the above items, I requested two additional items be added to the agenda for the May 23 meeting. The notes below are my preparation for those items.

### Public Outreach Subcommittee

As we near the August elections, the next phase of the Charter Review is to educate voters about our work. The Public Outreach subcommittee would aim to do this.

In my view, we need a subcommittee of three (3) members who are actively considering how to communicate the work of the Charter Review Committee to voters. The main charge of this subcommittee is to prepare a brief document that serves as an executive summary for voters. Additionally, the subcommittee would recommend how the Charter Review Committee can achieve effective voter education and outreach beyond just the document.

The document would explain the operation of the Charter Review Committee and the proposed charter amendments, including their merits. It would create a coherent summary of our work these past few months and provide a clear and concise explanation of proposed amendments to voters. The document could be available on the Charter Review website and other avenues for public distribution.

The importance of this outreach and education task dictates that we need a formal subcommittee seated rather than relying on fate and happenstance. A small, focused subcommittee consisting of Committee members with public relations and outreach experience would be of great value to this Committee. (For example, as an engineer, I have almost zero public outreach skills, which, unfortunately, is probably obvious. However, the output of this subcommittee would be very beneficial to me in communicating our Charter work to the public.)

## Ballot Drafting Subcommittee

To address ballot fatigue, we should select a Ballot Drafting Subcommittee responsible for drafting ballot language and selecting question order.

This committee's output would be essentially the August ballot. If the office of the law director is amenable, this subcommittee would work quite closely with the law director to draft ballot language.

Three (3) members should be sufficient. A small, focused group that could work quickly.

CHAPTER 3

# Meeting: June 27

WE HELD THE LAST SIGNIFICANT meeting on June 27, 2021. The August elections would be soon. Thus, this meeting would have the last substantive discussions on items of importance to the Charter. We thought the meetings might go months more, but by the end of June, the Committee had built consensus around major themes, and little work seemed to remain. My preparations for this meeting are the most extensive, with many more references than in previous writings.

## Appoint or Elect (Bureaucrats vs. Politicians)

An item before the Charter Review Committee is whether one or more Knox County offices (Law Director, Trustee, Register of Deeds, County Clerk, and Property Assessor), which are currently popularly elected, should instead be appointed by the Knox County Mayor, with possible consent from Commission. This document refers to these offices collectively as "Row Offices," where the discussions in the Appendix clarify this term.

## Evidence Does Not Support Appointment

The case for appointment lacks any compelling evidence. In research studies on government, the empirical evidence does not support a wholesale change in Knox County government from elected to appointed Row Offices (Deno & Mehay, 1987; Hoover, 2008; Lineberry & Fowler, 1967; MacDonald, 2008; Morgan & Kickham, 1999; Morgan & Pelissero, 1980; Rauch, 1994). While the research on the elect-appoint question is small, the reported outcomes agree that little to no differences exist along metrics such as fiscal management, performance efficiency, expenditure allocation, etc. This evidence begs the question, "What's the point? What problem does appointment actually solve?"

The theoretical argument is that politicians (elected offices) are motivated to win the next election, while bureaucrats (appointed offices) are motivated to avoid being fired.* While these motivations have good and bad traits, they essentially translate to politicians being more responsive to Voters while bureaucrats are more responsive to their bosses. A cynic might argue which is the lesser of two evils: politicians or bureaucrats; or as George Benard Shaw once said, "Democracy substitutes election by the incompetent many for appointment by the corrupt few" (Shaw, 2019).

---

* *This charged rhetoric is perhaps unfair to politicians and appointees and should maybe be toned down. The intent is to convey sentiment rather than absolute truth.*

## Personal Notes and Position Papers

Theoretically, the appointive process is devoid of politics. Practically, the official who has the power to appoint, as well as those who have the authority to confirm appointments, are heavily influenced by political forces (Group, 2000). The chaotic and dysfunctional appointive process at the federal level illustrates how politics plays a major role (Kalt, 2011). The federal process is further complicated by the "consent of the Senate" clause for appointments such that the appointed offices have become a political football and bargaining chip. Consider that over 18 months into his first term, more than 25% of President Obama's key policy-making positions had not yet been confirmed by the Senate (Kalt, 2011). Knox County would not be immune.*

While the federal government prefers the appointment process, the overwhelming majority of local governments throughout the United States are heavily biased toward elections, with nearly 176,000 elected state and county officials (Stolberg & Rutenberg, 2006). This fact is supported by the preference of our Founding Fathers for Federalism, where national and state (and local) governments share power—as a single centralized power (Berry & Gersen, 2008; Madison, 2016). In particular, early leaders such as Thomas Jefferson and later Andrew Jackson led the charge for more democracy

---

* *Some folks have argued that Mayoral appointments should have confirmation by the Commission (E. Board, 2012c). An unintended consequence is that the Commission could withhold key appointments to "bully" Mayoral action. The heavy hand of politics is never far in any form of government. The best-laid plans of mice and men often lead to simply choosing your poison. The confirmation process could potentially replace a grid of elected Row Offices with the gridlock of appointed department heads.*

at the local level, where government functions more directly impact the people's daily lives (Holgate, 2004).

Elections, rather than appointments, are the hallmark of American local government.

## Changing Knox County's Form of Government

The appointment of the Row Offices is, in essence, a wholesale change in Knox County's government. Whether for or against the amendment, one must acknowledge that enacting it would move Knox County away from a "Strong Commission" form of government to a "Strong Mayor" form. Recognizing this change is critical to understanding the potential impact and implications.

To understand the difference between Strong Commission and Strong Mayor, Appendix A illustrates various possible forms of county government, as adapted from the National Civic League (League, 2011). The offices in question are commonly known as "Fee Offices" since the Register of Deeds, County Clerk, and others collect fees for services such as registering real property titles, issuing marriage licenses, etc. In other situations, the term "Constitutional Offices" is used since the Tennessee Constitution explicitly creates the Trustee, Property Assessor, and others.

In this whitepaper, the term "Row Offices" refers to the entire set of offices to clarify potential ambiguity between "Fee" and "Constitutional" terms. Additionally, the term "Row Offices" better illustrates the relation of these offices to the Voter as these offices form a "Row" on an organizational chart.

Personal Notes and Position Papers

## Compelling History: Affirmation of Popular Elections

The popular election of Row Offices dates back to the second Tennessee Constitution of 1835 when Jacksonian Democracy was sweeping the nation (Jacoby, 1997). The popularity of Andrew Jackson ushered in increased democratization of the American political process, particularly at the local level. Before the Jacksonian movement, most local offices in Tennessee were appointed with minimal discretionary authority.

With the Jacksonian expansion of democracy, the Tennessee Constitution was rewritten in 1835 to change the Sheriff, Trustee, and Register of Deeds from appointed to elected offices (Vile & Byrnes, 1998). The Tennessee Legislature and later amendments to the Tennessee Constitution created the other Row Offices and established them as elected positions.

Some have suggested that the Row Offices' election—rather than appointment—is antiquated from a bygone time. However, the historical record decidedly tells a different story. Appointment is an antiquated concept long ago discarded by Tennesseans. Consider the initial conversion from appointment to election in 1835; a long and compelling history affirms the election of Row Offices:

- 1835 Tennessee Constitution; converts Sheriff, Trustee, and Register of Deeds from appointed offices to elected offices;
- 1870 Tennessee Constitution; post-Civil War rewrite to re-enter the Union reasserts election of Row Offices;
- 1978 Amendments; in the shadow of Watergate, elevate County Clerk and Property Assessor to Constitutionally elected offices and indirectly reaffirm the election of the other Row Offices;

- 1990 Knox County Charter; home rule definitively establishes election of Row Offices; and
- 2008 Charter Amendments; appointment rejected by 72% of voters, a clear mandate* for direct election (Ferrar, 2008).

This history ridicules the notion that the election of Knox County Row Offices is antiquated. Instead, it suggests the resilience of direct election and the clear preference of the Knox County Voter to elect Row Offices.

## Row Offices: Shared Executive Power Over the County Purse

The Strong Commission form of government places the primary responsibility for governing in the hands of the elected Commissioners as a body politic. Our Charter has established the Strong Commission (legislative body) as the preferred form of government in Knox County.

**Strong Legislative Branch, Embodied in the Commission**

The Charter (and Tennessee state law for other counties) primarily elevates the legislative body relative to the executive by dividing the executive across multiple Row Offices. As noted previously, the term Row Offices alludes to this division whereby the offices appear in a row on an organizational chart (Counties, 1999).

---

\* *Some folks have argued that the amendment's wording in 2008 unfairly biased the Voter. However, empirical evidence suggests that attempts at "ballot framing" by crafting the language on the ballot have little effect. See the work of Burnett and Kogan (Burnett & Kogan, 2010, 2012). The margins in the 2008 question are clearly well beyond any ballot-framing effects.*

The division of the executive into the Mayor, Trustee, Register of Deeds, Clerks, Sheriff, School Superintendent, and Property Assessor requires shared but distinct responsibilities for the executive's duties, specifically tax collection, property records, licensing, policing, education, etc. The offices have different lines of authority with almost zero overlap in responsibilities, which is essential for accountability to the Voter.

Such division spreads the powers of the executive over the Row Offices as opposed to consolidating them into the single office of the Mayor. This dilution of power to create a non-unified executive is not accidental but deeply intentional (Tarr, 2018) to subordinate the executive to the legislative body (Commission).

Interestingly, nearly every state in the union employs a division of the executive at both the state and county level using elected Row Offices (Holgate, 2004).

In Knox County, this subordination is not direct but indirect through the division of authority over the purse and the county's legal services. The Mayor serves as the county's principal financial officer and oversees non-legal services such as parks, roads, etc. However, the Row Offices execute the bulk of legal services such as tax collection, bond issuance, licensing, law enforcement, and other legal duties and services. With a bit tongue-in-cheek, one might say the Mayor is responsible for the finance and fun in the county while the Row Offices are responsible for the dirty work of taxation and licensing.

The executive branch's authority is not in the hands of a single individual, and with this division, the final authority on County policy rests in the Commission. To put it another way, the Knox County Mayor does not have unilateral authority.

The Mayor shares authority with the Row Offices and is ultimately subordinate to the Commission.

## Two-Person Rule: Heeding the "Nuclear Option" and Executive Review

The "Nuclear Option" is a euphemism for executive review. Judicial review is probably more familiar whereby a court interprets the constitutionality of a law and perhaps invalidates that law on constitutional grounds. By comparison, executive review—subject ultimately to judicial review—is the notion that the executive (the Mayor or Row Offices) has the power to interpret the law (Williams, 2006), Such interpretation may lead to selective enforcement* of particular laws or other discretionary actions.

While judicial review is commonly accepted, executive review is a bit more controversial but has recently come to the forefront. Consider the 2004 actions of the Mayor of San Francisco directing the County Clerk (appointed position) to make whatever changes were necessary "in order to provide marriage licenses on a nondiscriminatory basis, without regard to gender or sexual orientation" (Amar, 2009).

San Francisco County has a Strong Mayor form of government, and thus, the Mayor was able to act unilaterally to "legalize" gay marriage in San Francisco, although later court rulings (judicial review) invalidated the Mayor's actions. The

---

* *As an example, an attorney general, which may be thought as a Row Office, often employs such discretionary enforcement when deciding what cases to prosecute and to what level. Typically, budgetary pressures constrain such discretionary enforcement but political philosophies may come into play as well.*

division of the executive branch in Knox County requires a higher standard for executive review than in San Francisco County, as no individual has such unilateral power.

The Knox County Mayor cannot simply interpret the law and act unilaterally. Rather, actions like those in San Francisco would require explicit agreement between the Clerk and the Sheriff at a minimum but more practically tacit agreement with the Mayor and the Law Director. Such controversial ("nuclear option") actions require agreement between two or more elected offices.

While such situations are rare[*] (thus the term "nuclear option"), a divided executive across multiple elected offices has definite benefits for restraining unilateral action. By analogy, the US military employs the concept of a two-person rule for launching nuclear weapons. Essentially, if nuclear weapons are to be launched and thus annihilate a whole city, two individuals must concur as to the legitimacy of a launch order. Similarly, to the extent such review is possible, executive review requires two or more elected officials to concur in Knox County because of the division of the executive into the Mayor and Row Offices.

When executive review occurs, it is usually in dramatic fashion. At the federal level, a well-known abuse of executive review was the "Saturday Night Massacre," when President Richard Nixon removed a series of individuals from appointed positions as the Watergate Scandal boiled over. The strong unified executive at the federal level enabled Nixon to

---

[*] *Another example is the 2006 refusal of the Mayor of New York (Michael Bloomberg) to enforce the city's Equal Benefits Law, which extended city employment benefits to same-sex partners (Meletta, 2007).*

act without anyone intervening. This episode nearly threw our federal government into a Constitutional crisis. The non-unified executive of Knox County offers considerable guard against a rogue Nixon-like official.

The recent debate over placing budgetary requirements on the Row Offices is perhaps an illustration of executive review by the Law Director (Bailey, 2011; Ferrar, 2011a, 2011b). As evidenced by recent memoranda to this Committee, Commissioner Briggs outlined a legal path whereby the Row Offices could be brought under budgetary review by the Commission (Briggs, 2012a, 2012b).

The Law Director based on research from CTAS (Bailey, 2011; Ferrar, 2011a; Sullivan, 2011) disagreed with the Briggs memoranda.* With an agreement between the Mayor and the Row Offices, the Commission chose to heed the Law Director's advice. Thus, the Law Director, in essence, exercised executive review privileges. The Law Director could have equally rejected CTAS and favored the legal path of the Briggs memoranda. Such actions may have led to a court battle with potentially unknown results (possibly in favor or possibly against, i.e., judicial review).

The executive review suggests that the Row Offices affect Knox County's policy agenda, and the office of the Law Director is a prime example. The non-unified executive (Mayor, Trustee, Clerk, Register, etc.) in Knox County is not the result of a random archaic process but rather quite intentional and well thought out.

---

* A Machiavellian view of Knox County government might argue that the motivation for support of appointment of the Law Director might arise from such a disagreement.

## Shuffling the Deck Chairs While the Titanic Sinks

Changing the Row Offices from elected to appointed positions is like shuffling the deck chairs as the Titanic sinks. Obviously, such an action is a pointless effort that does not solve the real problem. This begs the question, what is the real problem that appointment is intended to solve, as Deputy Law Director David Buuck points out in his recent memo to this committee (Buuck, 2012). In light of the empirical evidence, the answer is nothing (Buuck, 2012; Deno & Mehay, 1987; Hoover, 2008; Lineberry & Fowler, 1967; MacDonald, 2008; Morgan & Kickham, 1999; Morgan & Pelissero, 1980; Rauch, 1994).

There is no evidence that the Row Offices would become more efficient, have less cronyism, or yield more accountability—as is often argued—if changed to Mayoral appointments. The only clear change is that the appointed offices would work to please the Mayor whereas the current elected offices work to please the Voters (Alesina & Tabellini, 2007). With no clear benefit, a real danger looms that a wholesale change in the form of County government may ignite unintended and detrimental consequences (Beeler, 2012; Donila, 2012).[*]

The Uniformed Officers Pension Plan (UOPP) comes to mind (Donila, 2011c). While the UOPP had overwhelming

---

[*] *Commissioner Mike Hammond recently warns of unintended consequences in regards to major changes in County government. Responding to Rep. Frank Niceley's efforts to eliminate the Metropolitan Planning Commission (MPC), Hammond says Niceley's proposal has "far-reaching ramifications." He thinks it should be "studied thoroughly and not just shot from the hip" (Donila, 2012). Such counsel is also wise with regard to the appoint-elect question, which is an even greater change in County government than the mere elimination of MPC.*

public support, its formation and funding implementation led to flawed results. An appointment amendment to the Charter demands careful and thorough consideration before, if at all, being placed on the ballot.

One might argue that the interest in moving to appointments is merely to give the appearance of doing something about an unavoidable situation. Mischief in government is unavoidable. Knox County is no exception. Appointments will not end mischief.

The list of appointed officials who have done wrong is long and is readily identified in past Knox County Mayoral appointments (Ferrar, 2011c). Illegal actions are not remedied by appointment and the National Civic League (League, 2011) warns charter committees against changing forms of government in response to short-term issues such as bad actors.

Neither appointment nor election ensures the proper character of government officials. Assuming so is merely shuffling the deck chairs.

## Summary

In summary, the empirical evidence does not support a wholesale change in Knox County government from elected to appointed Row Offices. Such a change would be a major realignment of County government and would go against compelling history that affirms popular election of the Row Offices. The design of the Knox County government intentionally divides the executive across the Mayor and Row offices to subordinate the executive branch to the Commission and to limit (i.e., diffuse to more than one office) the power of executive review. In light of the evidence, the efforts to move towards appointment is like shuffling the deck chairs on the Titanic.

## Fee Offices

One of my side conversations in the Committee was, "Why are people so afraid of putting something on the ballot?" This question centered around the fee offices. I remember being angry at the framing of the question. The language of "afraid" is a challenge charged with emotion. In my notes, I noted that "fear-mongering is a tool of thugs." This framing is a way to bully someone rather than to address their reasoning.

### Fear Mongering

An item before the Charter Review Committee is whether to change the Fee Offices from "Constitutional Offices" to "Charter Offices," the primary difference being eliminating the Salary Suit process.

Dr. Richard Briggs (Staff, 2012) questioned the courage of committee members who disagreed with his opinion. Such fear-mongering is a tool for those who stand on weak foundations. This is disappointing, as it comes from Dr. Briggs's usually articulate and intelligent mind.

### Salary Suit Background

Perhaps the best place to start is by explaining the Salary Suit process. Misunderstandings of the process and its role in the County government are probably at the heart of efforts to eliminate it.

David L. Page, Ph.D.

**Who Can File a Salary Suit? The Fee Offices.**

The Salary Suit process essentially applies to the following offices (*Tennessee County Government Handbook, County Technical Assistance Service*, 2010):*

- Sheriff,†
- County Clerk,
- Register of Deeds, and
- Trustee.

The common trait among these offices is that they collect fees for services rendered on behalf of the County. As a result, they are sometimes called "Fee Offices." One should notice that the following offices are excluded from the Salary Suit process:

- Law Director and
- Property Assessor.

Neither of these offices collects fees, so the check-and-balance of the Salary Suit is unnecessary. The question of

---

* *Other offices such as Clerk of Circuit Courts and Clerk of Criminal Courts are technically on this list as well. However, these offices are not under consideration for the potential Charter amendment before this Committee.*

† *The Sheriff's Office does submit a budget that is approved through Commission, but Tennessee Law allows for a Salary Suit if the Sheriff disagrees with the Commission budget. As an aside, Shelby County, which has eliminated Salary Suits through their Charter (Sec. 8.12), does still allow their Sheriff to file a Salary Suit (Sec. 8.13) (Shelby County Charter).*

whether or not an office is a Fee Office is a critical point to consider for the Salary Suit.*

**What Is a Salary Suit? The Fee Office Budget Negotiation.**

Like any County office, a Fee Office must have authorization to spend County money on salaries for deputies and assistants. In Knox County, such authorization can come from the Commission through the annual budget or from a court through a Salary Suit.

The Salary Suit is, in simple terms, the authorized salary budget for the Fee Office that establishes the number of deputies and assistants and their salaries. It is not the fee office's operating budget. The Suit only includes salaries, while operating expenses appear in the County budget. The fee offices' operating expenses, excluding salaries, are already included in the County's budget.

The Salary Suit is the last step in the budget authorization process, and in some cases, it may not be required.

First, the Fee Official (Trustee, Clerk, etc.) negotiates with the County Mayor about the number of deputies and assistants for the office and their associated compensation. If the Fee Official and the Mayor reach an agreement, the Fee Official may enter into a "Letter of Agreement" with the Mayor. This agreement is on a form approved by the State Comptroller and is filled with the court.

---

* *In 2011, Commissioner Briggs initiated a process to get rid of the Salary Suits. News reports (Bailey, 2011; Donila, 2011b; Ferrar, 2011a, 2011b) and legal briefs from Commission Briggs (Briggs, 2012a, 2012b) document this effort, which concluded with an opinion from the Law Director (Jarrett, 2011) that, in essence, amending the Charter would be required to eliminate the Salary Suits.*

David L. Page, Ph.D.

If the Fee Official and Mayor cannot agree, then the Salary Suit comes into play. The Fee Official must file a Salary Suit with the court to obtain authority to hire deputies and assistants. The Law Director would represent the Mayor, and the Fee Office would hire outside counsel to litigate (Jarrett, 2012).[*]

The court would listen to both sides—the Fee Office and the Mayor—and then rule on the number of deputies and assistants and salaries for the Fee Office. The court has the authority to set these salaries. This judicial oversight protects the services of the Fee Offices from being compromised by other fiscal needs of the County.

**How Does a Fee Office Pay Salaries? Fees Are Not Taxes.**

The Fee Offices collect fees for marriage licenses, real property titles, etc., and use these fees to pay the salaries of their offices. In essence, through the fee system, the Fee Offices are self-sustaining and, in most cases, do not require salary funding from the County general fund.[†] Excess fees that the offices collect beyond salaries are turned over and placed in the County general fund.

---

[*] In Knox County, the Mayor has rarely questioned the Salary Suits of the Fee Offices. According to Joe Jarrett, the Law Director's Office has not litigated a Salary Suit in the past four years. Additionally, there is some evidence that a Salary Suit has not been litigated in over 10 years in Knox County.

[†] In most counties throughout Tennessee, Court Clerks—particularly criminal courts—typically do not cover the operating salaries of their offices through collected fees due to the nature of the fees. An apt quote might be that it is easier to get blood from a turnip than to collect fees in criminal courts.

## Personal Notes and Position Papers

To illustrate, in 2010, the Offices collected $21.3 million in fees and spent $15.9 million on salaries (Donila, 2011b). The Offices thereby turned over nearly $6 million to the County. In business terms, the Fee Offices made a "profit" of $6 million for the County in 2010.* For perspective, the total Knox County budget is on the order of $700 million.

At this point, one should note the difference between "fees" and "taxes", which motivates the above business "profit" comparison. The difference is more than just semantics, where the purpose of the fee-tax charge is key to understanding (Henchman & Greaves, 2009).

Public authorities charge fees for rendering services to citizens or regulating their conduct. Fees cover the cost of providing those services or regulations. Taxes, on the other hand, are compulsory charges that confer no exclusive benefit to the payers. Taxes are assessments that raise money over what is needed to defray costs (Henchman & Greaves, 2009). Fees fund a specific government activity while taxes fund the government in general.

This difference is important to understanding why the Fee Offices need an independent process such as the Salary Suits to set salaries. The Fee Offices need to be able to set their staffing levels without Commission meddling to provide the services they are mandated to provide. However, the fee offices are not free to simply spend collected fees willy-nilly

---

* *Although the County is not a for-profit business, this business terminology is helpful to understand the fee system and the Fee Office salaries. As will be discussed later, the County government making a "profit" from services is, in my view, immoral, if not illegal.*

without a check and balance. The Salary Suit is the check and balance.

## How Does a Salary Suit Provide a Check and Balance? The Mayor's Role.

When operating correctly, the Salary Suit provides a check and balance by avoiding abuses in fee collection through judicial oversight. For proper functioning, the Mayor must play an important role. The key to that role is not to rubberstamp Fee Office budgets. The Mayor has two avenues to serve as a check over these salary budgets, and it is important that the Mayor exercise these avenues thoroughly.*

The first avenue is the court of public opinion. The Mayor must take the role of negotiating with the Fee Office seriously. If the Mayor sees some shenanigans during that negotiation, he should take his case to the public and use the bully pulpit to speak out against the Fee Office. The Mayor should ensure that he has the support of public opinion before taking the next avenue, i.e., going to court.

If the Mayor cannot sway the Fee Office to change their salaries via the weight of public opinion, then the Mayor must force the Fee Office to file a Salary Suit to protect the interests of the County. This second avenue ultimately puts the final decision in the hands of a judge.

While the Mayor's first avenue is political, this second avenue is hopefully more removed from politics (although admittedly not entirely removed). After hearing both the

---

* *The check and balance system has broken down until recently. The 2011 negotiations between the Mayor and the Register along with other Row Officers are a prime example of this check and balance system functioning properly (Ferrar, 2011b).*

Mayor's and the Fee Office's cases, the court decides the staffing and salary levels suitable for the operation of the Fee Office. The final court ruling serves as the authority for the Fee Official to hire assistants and deputies.

## Need for Salary Suits: Fees Should Not Be a Source of Revenue

Fees are not taxes. As such, fees should not be used by the County as a source of revenue for the general fund. Taxes are the fair and equitable mechanism for the County to raise revenue. Funding general operations on the backs of fee payers, however, is paving the "road to serfdom" and is a clear tyranny of the majority (Hayek, 1944).

Young folks getting married should not have to pay a fee for a marriage license to support building schools. Such a fee should simply cover the costs necessary for the government to provide the licensing service. Yielding the authority of the Fee Offices' budgets to the Commission is a strong temptation to change this equation.

Fee Offices that set their salaries have a unique incentive to ensure that the fees they collect cover the costs of operating their offices. An elected Fee Office that must request general funds from the Commission—above and beyond their collected fees—opens a wide door for potential challengers at the ballot box.

With Salary Suits, Fee Offices are highly motivated to, first, control salaries to fit within fee collection restraints and, second, turn over as much money from fees to the County general fund as possible. If these two objectives are met, they are huge political wins for Fee Office holders and, conversely, political bombshells for electoral opponents to lob if they are not met.

David L. Page, Ph.D.

Two important traits are also inherent to these objectives. The first trait is quality service to the public. The Fee Offices interact extensively with citizens, mainly through fee collection. As such, political self-interest encourages Fee Offices to maintain a high service standard and avoid the bureaucracy's malaise. If one compares the service they receive from the County Clerk to that of the US Post Office, one quickly understands the notion of bureaucratic malaise at the Post Office.

The second trait is equitable fee collection. A Fee Office that abuses fee collections with favoritism or prejudice soon faces electoral challenges.*

Also, the independence that the Salary Suit process affords the Fee Offices discourages situations where fees are squeezed to meet shortfalls in general funds. If the Commission controls the budgets of the Fee Offices, the political calculus changes. The Commission's focus is not on a particular Fee Office and the services it provides but rather on the entire

---

* *The 1998 election of Cathy Quist over Lillian Bean is perhaps an example of how the mischief of the Fee Office can bring down the strongest of political machines. Additionally, during the 2002 rerun between Quist and Bean, Quist's initial efforts at modernization also illustrate the need—and potential perils—for a Fee Office to be self-sustaining through fee collection (Henderson, 2002; Madison, 1999). While these campaigns had a fair amount of drama and intrigue, the Quist-Bean elections are an important example of the need for the Salary Suit process. By contrast, abuses in the solid waste department of Knox County languished for nearly seven years with little to no oversight (Donila, 2011a). Management of this department falls under a Mayoral appointment with salaries and contracts buried deep in the immense County budget.*

## Personal Notes and Position Papers

County budget. As a result, County fees are an easy temptation when revenue is tight.*

This temptation is precisely why the staffing of the Fee Offices is an executive issue with possible mediation from an impartial court, if necessary. Unlike other County departments, the Fee Offices provide direct services to citizens and charge fees in return, much like a business. A multi-person legislative body such as the Commission is ill-equipped to manage the business of the Fee Offices. The staffing levels of the Fee Offices are an executive issue and not a legislative issue.

At a very base level,† under the Salary Suit process, the Fee Offices (both the office holder and their staff) are strongly motivated to collect as many fees as possible and to do so with a smile on their faces. Their salaries and jobs depend on it. Under a Commission budget process, this motivation is removed and replaced by the varied and complicated interests of the multi-person Commission. This system pays the office holder and their staff regardless of how well they collect fees. Recall the Post Office.

Under the Salary Suit process, the buck stops with the office holder. Voters can readily discipline Fee Offices at the ballot box. Fee Offices cannot afford to offer poor service to citizens or to put minimal effort into collecting fees. Under

---

*A troubling trend has emerged recently where local governments are using fees to fill budget gaps since raising taxes has become quite unpopular (Follick, 2008; Segal, 2011; Skelton, 2007; Staff, 2007). Commission control over Fee Office budgets has potential pitfalls for such fee-tax manipulations.*

†*Self-interest may seem crude and base, but it lies at the heart of Adam Smith's "Invisible Hand" such that individuals seeking self-interest are a key driver to mutually beneficial outcomes.*

Commission-controlled salaries, blame is more complex to pinpoint. Shared responsibility across the Commission makes it challenging for Voters to discriminate, reducing accountability.

Commission budgetary control removes self-interest motivations in the Fee Office and introduces bureaucratic motivations. As will be discussed next, such bureaucracies within federal Fee Offices have proven extremely detrimental to the US Post Office and the US Patent and Trademark Office.

**Federal Fee Offices: The Case Against Legislative Fee Budgets**

The federal government does not refer to them as such, but the US Post Office and the US Patent and Trademark Office are two examples of Fee Offices at the federal level. Both of these offices should serve as a warning to Knox County of the potential for abuse when the legislative branch of government controls fee budgets.

*US Post Office: Congressional Meddling*

First, consider the US Post Office. The Post Office's woes are well-documented and probably well-known to most folks. However, cataloging this office's near brink of collapse is worth repeating, as congressional budget control lies at the heart of the mismanagement.

Congress has its hands deeply embedded in the postal mess and the widely held belief that the Postal Service is on the brink because it's outdated or because of Internet competition is not supported by the facts (Greenhouse, 2011; Keane, 2012; Rolando, 2011).*

Consider that the Post Office between 2007 and 2010 made a net operational profit of over $60 0 million (Rolando, 2011). The red ink, however, comes mainly from a 2007 Congressional mandate to aggressively pre-fund future retiree health benefits, which currently translates to payments of about $6 billion annually (Greenhouse, 2011; Keane, 2012). The pre-funding mandate—not competition from the Internet—is crippling the budgets of the Post Office. Congress has artificially created a budget problem for the Post Office.

As Joe Nocera of the New York Times opines, "Congress just can't stop meddling" (Nocera, 2012). The Congressional pre-funding requirement has no reasonable basis in fact and is wholly unnecessary (Rolando, 2011). With that said, the Post Office has developed a five-year plan to overcome its woes, but again, Congressional meddling, particularly with the proposal to close the rural office, has not allowed a sustainable path (Greenhouse, 2011; Keane, 2012).

The multi-person body of a legislature (e.g., Congress or Commission) is ill-suited to manage a Fee Office such as the Post Office. With the buck spread over various legislators' interests rather than stopping at the top, political decisions—such as grossly overfunding future benefits—rather than operational decisions—such as closing unneeded rural offices—rule the day.

---

* *Anecdotally, the Post Office has survived other technology challenges similar to the internet such as the telegraph and telephone. Experts suggest that a viable path forward for the Post Office is possible (Greenhouse, 2011; Keane, 2012; Nocera, 2012).*

Knox County should heed the lesson of the mismanagement of the Post Office by Congress as a reason not to allow the Commission to manage the staffing levels of the Fee Offices.

*US Patent and Trademark Office: Robbing Peter to Pay Paul*

As an engineer, I am personally saddened by the mismanagement of the Patent Office. This situation has crippled America's competitive edge, where intellectual property is perhaps a major cornerstone of our economy.

Like the Post Office, the US Patent and Trademark Office is supposed to be self-sustaining through the fees collected for patent and trademark issuances. Unfortunately, like the Post Office, the Patent Office is not meeting operational expenses from these fees, and the blame lies squarely on Congress's shoulders.

The main reason is that Congress is "robbing" the Patent Office.

In 1991, the Patent Office became self-sustaining, and taxpayers no longer funded the agency with their tax dollars. Rather, the Office started financing itself through collected user fees. Unfortunately, from 1991 to 2004, Congress diverted more than $650 million in collected patent fees to unrelated programs across the federal government (Chartrand, 2004). The fees collected by the Patent Office are just too enticing for the sticky hands of Congress.

This Congressional raiding of Patent Office fees has come at a serious cost. The agency is simply incapable of keeping pace with the volume and complexity of the patent applications it receives. Without proper funding, the Patent Office has been unable to hire a sufficient number of qualified patent reviewers to keep pace. In 2009, the backlog has grown to more than 1.2 million applications, an estimated six-year

## Personal Notes and Position Papers

backlog (Schmid, 2009). This situation does not have to be. If the Patent Office could keep the fees it collected, the office would be able to hire enough reviewers to meet demand.

Folks who understand the patent process (Editorial, 2006; Schmid, 2009; Schmid & Poston, 2009) are deeply concerned about the problems this Congressional diversion of fees is causing. For example, patents that are not novel and should have never been issued are slipping through the cracks (Editorial, 2006).* More patent applications are filed daily, yet congressional plundering hampered the Patent Office's staffing levels.

In Knox County, the fee revenues of the Fee Offices would be a tempting source of funds for the Commission. Unfortunately, the Commission's diversion of fees would yield problems similar to those with county services as in the Patent Office. The Salary Suit process demarks a distinct line between the Commission and the Fee Offices to avoid this robbing-Peter-to-pay-Paul problem.

### Summary

Some have suggested that the Salary Suit is an antiquated system. That belief is fundamentally not true. The Salary Suit is quite a sophisticated system that reduces abuses and mismanagement of fee collections. This system, however, requires

---

*A notorious example of a patent that should not have been granted is a 1999 patent for peanut butter and jelly sandwiches, which the J. M. Smucker Co. acquired and attempted to enforce. Later court rulings, however, struck down the viability of the patent ("Court rejects J. M. Smucker's PB&J patent," 2005). The lack of qualified reviewers in the Patent Office has led to such patents slipping through the system.

that each actor (the Fee Official, the Mayor, and the courts) take their responsibilities seriously. Fees are not taxes, and special protections such as the Salary Suit are necessary to ensure that fee collection does not become a tyrannical stand-in for tax collection. Knox County would be wise to look at the mismanagement of federal Fee Offices such as the US Post Office and the US Patent and Trademark Office to see the pitfalls that can occur with legislative meddling.

CHAPTER 4

# Conclusions

**M**ANY OF THE CONCLUSIONS already appear within the chapters above. I have little to add beyond those discussions. The writings here are now over 10 years old, and my compulsion to compile them into a published work is more selfish than altruistic in that I wanted to create—invoking the flair of Nicholas Negroponte[*]—a physical reference of "atoms" on my bookshelf beyond the digital files of "bits" on my computer hard drive.

I am a bookophile. I prefer real physical books over electronic copies or facsimiles. I enjoy holding the book in my hands and turning the pages. I love to skim the contents and skip through the figures. This personal joy has led me to publish this collection of papers. I am doubtful that the collection

---

[*] Negroponte wrote a non-fiction book (Negroponte, 1995), published in 1995, about the rise of digital technologies and their possible future. He introduces the notion of a world made of "atoms," which are the foundational particles of our physical world, and one made of "bits," which are the foundational units of the virtual worlds.

will ever prove helpful, but I am hopeful that the opinions I have expressed here may give insight into one citizen's engagement in local government.

My conclusions are thus more of a challenge to the reader, and that challenge is to be engaged—to be thoughtful, to stand up and be heard. I am reminded of the famous Norman Rockwell painting shown below, which depicts a town hall meeting where a speaker stands, bracing his hands with courage on the bench before him, to express his views to the assembly. This painting is perhaps the most appropriate manner to conclude this book.

Figure 1. Norman Rockwell. "Freedom of Speech." Office of War Information, CC BY 2.0 <https://creativecommons.org/licenses/by/2.0>, via Wikimedia Commons.

# Acknowledgments

I WANT TO THANK my wife, Lisa, and my daughter, Grace, for their love and support on so many levels. They have supported my crazy ideas to pursue a wide range of interests over the years from politics to tech startups to poker player to newspaper columnist to book author to self-publisher and to a variety of hobbies in between. This book adds to that list. As such, it is my second self-published work, and Lisa and Grace have suffered, perhaps too much, through each step of the process.

When I first drafted the notes and papers compiled here, Grace was only five years old. After putting her to bed each night around 8:00 PM, I would start working on the research and writing the essays. Today, however, she is a senior in high school and no longer goes to bed so early. We both work late into the night as partners in crime—her on school work and me on writing.

Lisa keeps us both grounded. As a mother and wife, she is a constant support, not just with her generosity but also her spirit. She sees the world differently, and her perspective challenges me toward a more well-rounded view. I am grateful to her and Grace for their kindness and patience. Thank you, Lisa and Grace.

I am also grateful to the many friends and colleagues who have shaped the discussions, arguments, and conclusions in these pages. My inbox is full of old emails from 2012 with comments and feedback on early drafts, partial thoughts, and rabbit trails that have found their way into the somewhat coherent expositions in this book.

One of those colleagues is Andreas Koschan. He was a mentor during my Ph.D. graduate work at the University of Tennessee. From time to time, we would have lunch together, and politics would be a common topic of discussion. He also invited me to "Global Hour," a weekly discussion group hosted at the International House on UT's campus. This international perspective on global politics gave me new insights into local politics that have impacted me. Thank you, Dr. Koschan.

A challenge I faced when serving on the Committee was that I struggled from time to time with public speaking. In general, I'm comfortable as a speaker, but I can tear up and cry easily when discussing topics I have strong convictions or passions about. This challenge is one that I have had difficulty with even today. My crying seems inappropriate and mismatched to my facial affect at the moment. I am a bit embarrassed by the situation as most folks become uncomfortable when they see a grown man of 240 pounds with a 5-foot, 11-inch frame crying. I have dealt with this issue for nearly 20 years, and as a result, I have developed multiple strategies to hide or disguise the tears.

However, the televised coverage of the Committee exacerbated the issue, and my response was to throw myself deeper into drafting my thoughts and outlining lines of debate before each meeting. This new strategy led me to engage more deeply in the writings presented here. In an odd way, I am thankful for this "crying" challenge as it made me a more thoughtful representative for the folks of Knox County.

Speaking of Knox County, I must also thank Brad Anders, who in 2012 served as the Commissioner of the Sixth

District—my commissioner. I have known Brad since we first met at the Karns Republican Club, and he was kind enough to appoint me to serve on this Committee. Thank you, Brad.

Finally, I must thank my late mother, Shirley Page, and my late father, Bob Page, who instilled in my brother, Dan, and me the importance of being engaged citizens. My mother was a Republican, and my father was a Democrat, yet our house was never divided. Thank you, Mom and Dad.

# Appendix

THE ELEMENTS OF THIS APPENDIX serve to further explain elements of the prior Charter and also include some important question and answer dialogues. The next section looks at different forms of local government that emphasis different strengths of the executive and legislative bodies. Subsequent sections look at the debates surrounding Knox County's specific issues within these frameworks.

## Forms of Local Government

The figures (Figs. A.1-A.3) on the following pages show organizational charts for common forms of local government. At the top is the Voter, to whom, ultimately, each form is held accountable. The relative size of the boxes indicates the level of responsibility to the Voter while the connecting lines denote reporting authority. A connecting line to the Voter indicates direct election, while a connecting line between two offices indicates appointment.

The "Row Offices" represent offices such as Trustee, Sheriff, Register, etc. The organizational charts illustrate the term as these offices appear across a common row. The Knox County form of government most closely follows Fig. A.2, Strong Commission.

The various forms in Figs. A.1-A.3 have varying levels of authority associated with each office. Typically, the direct election of an office supports a significant level of authority as the voice of the Voter is more directly represented in such offices. Meanwhile, offices further down the chart and further away from the voter have supposed lesser authority, at least from an electoral mandate perspective.

These charts are, in some sense, idealized, as most practical forms of local government are often a mixture of forms.

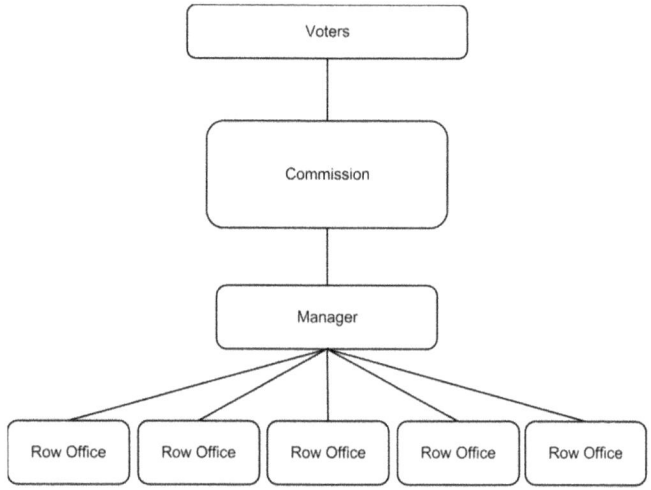

Figure A.1. Commission-manager form of county government. (Adapted from (League, 2011).) The Commission appoints a county manager to run the executive functions of government. The Knox County School Board follows this model to a certain degree. This form is rare in county governments in the US. Two noteworthy examples, however, are Santa Clara County, CA ("Silicon Valley") and Durham County, NC ("Research Triangle"). Santa Clara appoints a County Manager but elects a Sheriff and Assessor. Durham also has an appointed County Manager but elects Row Offices (Sheriff, Register of Deeds, and Clerk of Court).

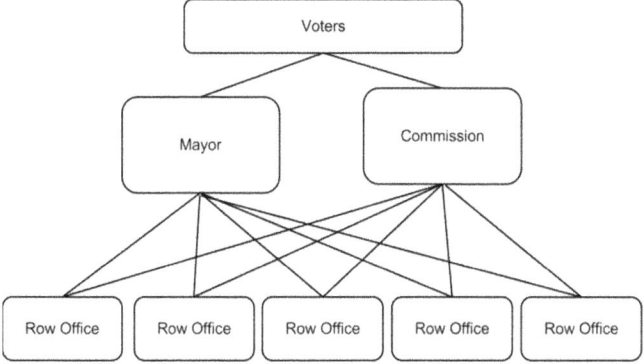

Figure A.2. Strong Mayor form of county government. (Adapted from (League, 2011).) The Voter elects both the Mayor and the Commission. The Mayor appoints the Row Offices while the Commission typically has consent review of the appointments.

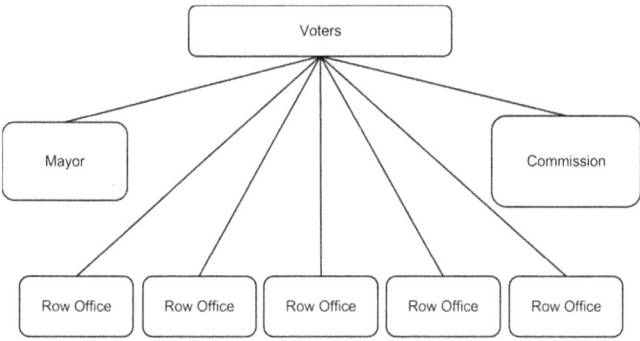

Figure A.3. Strong commission form of county government. (Adapted from (League, 2011).) Current form in Knox County. Mayor, Commission, and Row Offices are popularly elected by Voters. The Commission has a strong presence in this form of government as the executive branch is divided across the Mayor and Row Offices, which are separately accountable to Voters.

David L. Page, Ph.D.

# Common Questions for Appoint-Elect Debate

The following list of questions provides a brief overview of some common arguments in the appoint-elect debate.

*Q1:* Doesn't an appointment yield a more qualified candidate, while an election produces a better campaigner?

The fundamental fallacy in this question is that a qualified candidate and a good campaigner are mutually exclusive and that Voters cannot discern between the two traits.

Perhaps more importantly, the question assumes that appointed positions such as Law Director, Trustee, or other Row Offices do not require political skill as part of their qualifications. One needs to look no further than the Superintendent of Schools (an appointed position in Knox County) to understand how much political savvy (i.e., a good campaigner) appointed offices often require. The public forum of government requires "good campaigners" at almost every level, particularly at the level of the Row Offices.

To suggest otherwise is to deny the political nature of the Row Offices, whether appointed or elected.

To put a face to this line of argument, Donald Rumsfeld (appointed Secretary of Defense) was more than qualified (quite a resume, including former Secretary of Defense under President Ford) but seemingly lacked political finesse (Birnbaum, 2001). As a result, his effectiveness in office was severely hampered as he became a lightning rod in the Bush administration (Stolberg & Rutenberg, 2006).

The history of executive appointments at the Presidential level is one of preferring political backgrounds as opposed to "most qualified." A 2010 report from the GAO found that the appointment process may jeopardize merit-based hiring practices in general (Yager, 2010).

Additionally, as the 1989 Volcker Commission report illustrated, political patronage is rampant in Presidential appointees. This means that appointments are not only politically charged and often lack merit, but the amount of money one gives to a Presidential campaign may determine what appointment a person receives.

Local government is not immune to the politicization over the merit of appointments and political patronage. If one scans the Mayoral appointments in the City of Knoxville over the past few years or even the Gubernatorial appointments at the state level, political background is often more important than most qualified.

It's a naive belief that appointment lacks politics and yields a more qualified official to serve in office.

***Q2:*** *Don't the events of the last five years in Knox County with the indictment of a former Trustee demonstrate the need for an appointment?*

An appointment will not eliminate bad actors from the political scene.

Appointment is not a panacea, particularly as protection against illegal acts. The list of appointed officials who have done wrong is long and is readily identified in the past Knox County Mayoral appointments (Ferrar, 2011c). Illegal actions are not remedied by appointment.

Further, the National Civic League strongly warns county charter committees to resist changing forms of government in response to bad actors (League, 2011). Political immediacy is often blinding to a country's true needs. At the end of the day, any system of government will eventually witness acts of corruption and abuses of power on the part of individuals and organizations (Mingus, 2007). Democracy is not perfect, but it is the best that we have.

To paraphrase John Adams, one of our Founding Fathers, our Charter form of government requires a moral people (Adams, 1798a). When the moral code of individuals breaks down, the consequences are high in government, regardless of whether they are elected (Bailey, 2012; Sumerford, 2010) or appointed (E. Board, 2012a; Donila, 2011a; Ferrar, 2011c). The only solution to bad actors is the people's eternal vigilance. Changing from elect to appoint merely shuffles the deck chairs and solves nothing.

***Q3**: Why should we elect offices that do not play a part in forming county policy?*

The Row Offices do play a major role in county policy. To say that they don't is wrong.

Consider the Law Director. Policy disagreements between the Law Director and Commissioners have often yielded dramatic moments in Knox County over the past few years (Donila, 2011b; Sullivan, 2011). The Law Director has a strong hand in forcing policy agendas through his willingness (or unwillingness) to defend court challenges robustly or through his interpretation of the law (state, Charter, etc.).

Additionally, the other Row Offices are essentially in charge of Knox County's financial purse, and the licensing and recording services they provide to Voters are a direct reflection of their interpretation of state law and county ordinances. In other words, they interpret and implement policy.

Such interpretation at the county level is perhaps best illustrated when, in 2004, the San Francisco County Clerk established a major policy agenda by issuing same-sex marriage licenses (Marinucci, 2004).

*Q4:* *Wouldn't an appointment provide greater accountability?*

Presidents come and go, but J. Edgar Hoover was a constant. The veil of a bureaucracy can hide many a sin, as Hoover's grip over the FBI illustrates. Others, such as Admiral Hyman Rickover in the US Navy, illustrate how bureaucrats often wield more power than their elected bosses (Lewis, 1980). Appointments do not increase accountability.

An example that is closer to home is the notorious Andrew Johnson Building. Some folks have argued the need for more accountability in the administration of Knox County Schools, and they have asked, "Has the appointment of the Superintendent increased accountability as to what goes on in the Andrew Johnson Building?"

Also, the Row Offices have separate and distinct responsibilities, which Voters can clearly distinguish. The lines of authority do not overlap, and voters can readily sanction individual row offices at the ballot box. This unbundling of the executive branch into the Mayor and Row Offices clarifies lines of authority and provides great accountability. If the Mayor appoints the Row Offices, a vote for the Mayor is markedly crude as Voters would have to average their experience with Row Offices, reducing accountability (Berry & Gersen, 2008).

To clarify, if one goes to the Clerk's office to renew a driver's license and must wait hours, then Voters know that the Clerk is responsible and can sanction at the next election. If one goes to do a title search on real property and the staff is rude and unhelpful, then Voters know to sanction the

Register of Deeds at the next election. Elections increase accountability.*

**Q5: *Isn't the election of the Row Offices an antiquated system, particularly the salary suits?***

The history of Tennessee and Knox County, from the second state Constitution in 1835 to the County Charter in 1990, represents a series of continuous affirmations by Voters for the election of the Row Offices. This history is compelling evidence of the resilience of elections over appointment rather than an indication of antiquity.

The salary suits are beyond the scope of this whitepaper and outside the question of appointment or election. That said, a misunderstanding of their function might lead one to conclude they are antiquated.

However, a better understanding reveals the true importance of salary suits as they deal with the allocation of fees, not taxes. A dangerous trend is evolving where fees are used to raise revenues, not taxes (Henchman & Greaves, 2009; Moon, 2009; Segal, 2011).

This is dangerous because governments are not profit-based businesses, and fees should not be used to raise revenue. Fees are not paid by everyone, and if they are used as a revenue source, they are, in essence, an unfair, non-distributive tax.

---

* An example where appointment led to reduced accountability is the 2011 problems with the solid waste office in Knox County (Donila, 2011a). One might argue that because an appointed department head oversaw this office accountability slipped. As Knox County Commission Chairman Mike Hammond said, "It's obvious to me that this department was out of control" (Donila, 2011a).

**Q6**: *Doesn't the business model of a CEO (Mayor) appointing department heads (Row Offices) lead to better government?*

Ironically, in the business model, the CEO is appointed, too. The CEO model would be more like a commission-manager form of county government where the Commission would appoint the Mayor.

Additionally, the government is not a business. No business (that I am aware of) has the authority to impose taxes to raise revenue. Taxation requires elected representation rather than appointed fiat.

To paraphrase Jeff Birnbaum, businesses care about profits; governments care about process. The bottom line measures business success, while success in government is more elusive (Birnbaum, 2001).

Anecdotally, Barnes and Noble's bookshelves are filled with hundreds of books about motivating employees, hiring and firing, and other business matters. None of these business books deal with governmental matters where "the bulk of employees cannot be motivated or fired" (Birnbaum, 2001). This charged language illustrates the difference between market and government jobs.*

The motivation levels of federal employees are quite notorious, with the Post Office serving as the prime example (Abraham et al., 2009). Consider that the Post Office is operating at a multi-billion-dollar deficit—that's a Billion with a big B!

---

* *This whitepaper would be remiss not to note that the vast majority of Knox County employees are highly motivated for the public good.*

If one compares Knox County's fee offices with federal "fee" offices such as the Post Office and Patent and Trademark Office, the efficiency of the elected Knox County fee offices is quite dramatic. The CEO model is unlikely to lead to a better government. The election of Fee Officials yields quality results in both services and budgets.

**Q7: Was the appointment amendment in 2008 defeated because of the biased wording on the ballot?**

In 2008, Knox County Voters clearly rejected the amendment for the mayoral appointment of Row Offices by 72% (Ferrar, 2008). However, some folks have argued that the wording on the ballot used charged language to trick Voters.

In the research literature, "ballot framing" describes deliberate attempts by officials and special interest groups to shape the language of ballot measures to bias the outcome. On the contrary, the evidence suggests that such efforts are highly unlikely to change outcomes (Burnett & Kogan, 2010), and the 72% margin is clearly above any potential ballot framing noise.

**Q8: Aren't the elected Row Offices nests for cronyism?**

This argument is relatively weak as the potential for cronyism is shifted up the ladder from the Row Offices to the Mayor under an appointment model. The recent botched appointment of the Finance Director demonstrates vividly that mayoral appointments are not impervious to cronyism (E. Board, 2012a, 2012b).

Scanning news accounts throughout the US, executive appointments are clearly no stranger to cronyism (Board, 1995; Craig, 2011; Johnston, 1996; Sack, 1995; Stewar, 2011). The worst offender is Marion Barry, former Mayor of DC and current council member. In referring to charges of cronyism,

Barry is quoted as saying, "To the victor goes the spoils" (Craig, 2011).

Nests of cronyism are unlikely to be solved by transitioning from elected to appointed Row Offices. The nature of cronyism has little to do with appointment or election but rather with human nature and power.* Term limits are the more likely remedy for cronyism. Knox County should give sufficient time to let term limits play out and weed out cronyism through attrition.

***Q9**: Wouldn't Knox County save money by eliminating redundancy across the Row Offices?*

Alleghany County (Pittsburgh) in Pennsylvania began a phased process of reducing their elected Row Offices from ten (10) to four (4) by 2008. The estimated savings is $1M annually ("Onorato Presents 2009 Comprehensive Fiscal Plan," 2008). This number initially seems quite amazing until one looks under the hood.

First, Alleghany's total annual budget for 2008 was $762M. So, for all the trouble (a nearly three-year effort), Alleghany saved 0.1% of its annual budget. Second, they simply consolidated Row Offices. Alleghany still retains four elected Row Offices, which is more in line with Knox County. Finally, the estimated $1M per year is reported by the County Mayor in a press release without detailed substantiation. Thus, the

---

* *On a personal note, I have worked at the University of Tennessee and the US Department of the Navy. Nests of cronyism and favoritism are not solely housed under the organizational charts of elected officials. Merit often takes a backseat to who you know.*

Alleghany case offers little credence to the savings argument for Knox County.

Following the experience of Alleghany, Cuyahoga County in Ohio adopted a new charter in 2009, which mandated a reduction in county operating costs by 15% through the consolidation of Row Offices from eleven (11) to just one (1). While Cuyahoga should be applauded for putting their money where their mouth is in their charter, the hoped-for savings have yet to materialize. These savings have proved elusive and difficult to achieve (Counties).

In light of these attempts at savings in Alleghany and Cuyahoga, arguments that the appointment of Row Offices would generate savings in Knox County seem inadequate.*

**Q10:** *Shouldn't we just put it on the ballot and let the Voters decide?*

As we have seen with the UOPP, casually formulating Charter amendments and simply placing them on the ballot is dangerous. This committee's role is to thoroughly vet each proposal to ensure the county's long-term interests are considered.

This Committee's charge is not to rubber stamp every idea floated but to act as a sortition jury to thoroughly vet each proposal. This Committee must have a robust (and perhaps even passionate) debate on each controversial amendment.

---

*Another point to consider is the notion of "public choice" where the division of the executive into the Row Offices pits these offices to some level of competition with each other for Voter approval. The research of Vincent Ostrom (Ostrom, 2008; Ostrom & Ostrom, 1971) outlines this notion where he argues that such competition in the public arena mirrors market competition in the private arena. Thus, this competition helps to squeeze out inefficiencies in the Row Offices.*

Personal Notes and Position Papers

Then, the Committee must make a well-informed decision on whether to put the amendment before the Voters.

The Voters are relying on this Committee as selected decision makers to do proper due diligence—to do our homework. We must rise to that call and not simply cast off our responsibilities with an unvetted motion to put a question before the Voters.

**QII**: *Isn't it easier to fire an appointed department head than to wait four years to sanction an elected official?*

Yes, but that is not necessarily a good thing.

There is no doubt that when an elected official participates in illegal acts, the public's inability to "fire" that official immediately is troublesome. Unfortunately, this inability is a necessary evil of representative democracy.

The opposite face of this coin is that an elected official's unpopular—but not illegal—acts also do not allow immediate termination. This fact goes to the core of representative democracy.

An official who takes steps that are perhaps in the long-term best interest of the County but may not be the most popular one has the security of his four-year term of office to encourage statesmen-like behavior rather than reactionary behavior.

The case of Bill Lockett is perhaps the motivation for this question (Sumerford, 2010) While no one disputes the former Law Director's guilt, using his case to argue for appointment is ill-advised. After all, a thoughtful person would not use Richard Nixon to argue that the US President should be appointed.

Bad actors are troublesome when they sneak into elected office. As Commissioner Ed Shouse said following the Lockett situation, "It is something that happened, and those of us who are in the public eye, particularly those running for elected office like this, we cannot have these things in our background and expect to serve the public as we should" (Sumerford, 2010).

The hope of a representative democracy is that without public support, elected officials have little effective authority, regardless of when the next election cycle occurs. An official's legitimacy is indirectly tied to popular support.

As the evidence mounted, both Nixon and Lockett became personae non-gratae, which hampered their ability to effectively perform their offices' functions. As their ineffectiveness became self-evident, they both resigned—a painful process for Voters to endure but a necessary evil in a representative democracy.

Illegal actions are irrelevant to the question of appointment or election.

## *Q12:* Doesn't appointment lead to greater transparency?

It is unlikely that the appointment process will introduce a whole new level of politics into the Row Offices, which is not visible to the public. The politics of appointment are often behind closed doors, where deals are cut with private discussions—beyond the reach of Sunshine Laws—on public issues. Appointments do not remove politics from the Row Offices but instead remove the Voters.

Political patronage is another new component that appointment introduces. While campaign finance laws yield some insight into patronage, the vast majority of tit-for-tat deals go undocumented. Patronage is a backroom process that is not transparent.

Appointments are not devoid of politics and do not increase transparency.

Personal Notes and Position Papers

## Common Questions for Salary Suit Debate

The following list of questions provides a brief overview of some common arguments in the Salary Suit debate. Some of these questions and associated answers are similar to those in the Appoint-Elect Debate above. I have repeated them here for completeness.

*Q1:* Shelby County has done away with Salary Suits in their Charter. Shouldn't Knox County follow Shelby County's lead?

To be clear, Shelby County has not done away with Salary Suits entirely. Shelby has eliminated Salary Suits for the Fee Offices. However, the Sheriff can still file a Salary Suit if so desired, although the form is much more restricted than that allowed by the Tennessee Constitution. Also, Shelby County still has Constitutional Offices, such as the court clerks that still have the authority to file Salary Suits as they fall outside the authority of the Shelby Charter (*Shelby County Charter*).

That said, simply because Shelby County has taken this avenue, it offers little convincing support for Knox County to do so. In particular, the amendments that eliminated Salary Suits in Shelby County have only been in effect since 2010. With only two years passed, no empirical evidence is available to suggest whether the Shelby County approach is good or bad. The jury is still out on Shelby County's decision to eliminate Salary Suits.

In essence the Shelby County example only answers the question of "how" to eliminate the Salary Suits but offers no clear answer for the more important question of "why."

*David L. Page, Ph.D.*

**Q2:** *Doesn't the events of the last five years in Knox County with the indictment of a former Trustee demonstrate the need for Commission oversight? (Bailey, 2012)*

Commission approval of budgets will not eliminate bad actors. As anecdotal evidence, consider the unfortunate P-card scandal of recent history, which sadly culminated in the conviction of Cynthia Finch (Ferrar, 2011c). More recently, the mismanagement of the solid waste department clearly illustrates that mischief is not solved by Commission oversight (Donila, 2011a).

Commission oversight of Fee Office salaries offers no more protection against illegal acts than the current judicial oversight afforded by the Salary Suit process. To paraphrase John Adams, one of our Founding Fathers, our Charter form of government requires a moral people (Adams, 1798b). When the moral code of individuals breaks down, the consequences are high in government.

**Q3:** *Aren't the Fee Offices where all the money problems are throughout the counties in Tennessee, particularly Knox County?*

Yes. As most auditors would agree, the answer to this question is fairly obvious. The Fee Offices are the point where money enters the Knox County coffers. Until that money goes into a bank account where tracking is more transparent, misbehavior is a ready temptation.

This problem is inherent to human nature rather than a structural problem of the Salary Suit process. The point where money exchanges hands is the most vulnerable for abuse in any system. Thus, the Fee Offices tend to be where money issues arise rather than in other departments such as the parks department.

Eliminating the Salary Suit process in Knox County will not eliminate the money temptations in the Fee Offices. Ironically, eliminating the Suits will lure the hands of the Commission into the fee pot, thereby expanding the realm of money mischief.

**Q4:** *Wouldn't including Fee Office salaries in the Mayor's budget provide greater accountability to Voters?*

The Mayor's 2012-2013 budget is over 500 pages long. That enormous document makes it quite a challenge to identify a particular office's staffing levels and salaries compared to the typically three—or four-page documents of the Fee Office Salary Suits.

Last year, Mayor Burchett and the Fee Offices, led by Register Sherry Witt, negotiated a compromise whereby the Fee Offices filed either a Salary Suit or a letter of agreement outlining personnel costs. This document was submitted to both the Mayor's office and the Commission during the budget process (Ferrar, 2011b).

Mayor Burchett and Register Witt should be applauded for these negotiations, which are a textbook example of how the Salary Suit process should work. This compromise increased the Salary Suit process's transparency and accountability to Voters. Burying the results of their negotiations in a 500-page budget would do little to serve the interests of openness.

**Q5:** *Isn't the Salary Suit process an outdated and antiquated system?*

This question results from a misunderstanding of the Salary Suit process. Once one realizes that the Salary Suit protects the abuse of the fee collection process from the Commission, one begins to realize that the Salary Suit is quite well thought out. This statement is not an indictment of the Commission but rather an understanding that the Commission's interests encompass the entire County government rather than a single Fee Office.

Congress's abuses of the US Post Office and the US Patent and Trademark Office clearly indicate the importance of the Salary Suits and the independence they afford the Fee Offices. To suggest that the Salary Suit process is outdated and old-fashioned is simply misguided.

## *Q6:* Shouldn't we just put it on the ballot and let the Voters decide?

As we have seen with the UOPP, formulating Charter amendments and simply placing them on the ballot is dangerous.* The role of this Committee is to thoroughly vet each proposal to ensure that the county's long-term interests are considered.

This Committee's charge is not to rubberstamp each idea floated but rather to act as a sortition jury to thoroughly vet each proposal. This Committee must have a robust (and perhaps even passionate) debate on each controversial amendment. Then, the Committee must make a well-informed decision on putting the amendment before the Voters.

The Voters rely on this Committee to do proper due diligence—to do our homework. We must rise to that call and not

---

* *The general consensus among Voters, based on the passing of the UOPP, is that the spirit of the UOPP is a good thing and desirable. However, as this Committee has debated, the implementation of the UOPP through the inflexible language of the UOPP amendment has led to detrimental consequences.*

simply cast off our responsibilities with an unvetted motion to put a question before Voters.

For good or for bad, most Voters will employ rational ignorance on many of the amendments that this Committee proposes. The potential benefit of a single amendment to an individual Voter most likely will not exceed the cost necessary to motivate the average Voter to educate oneself on the minute details of an amendment.

Thus, our job is to thoroughly hash out the details of proposed amendments—to do the grunt work for the Voters—and to ensure the amendments lead to good government.

Our job is not simply to put amendments on the ballot; our job is to test them.

## Proposed Amendments to Article IX of the Charter

During the review, I proposed one amendment, but as I recall, I am unsure that it ever came to a vote before the committee. Based on my experience sitting on the committee, the following draft is my proposal to amend the charter review committee's makeup and manner.

At the committee's first meeting, I saw that none of the members seemed prepared for the process. Selecting a chairman was an awkward first step. Additionally, the large number of committee members made the process unwieldy and difficult to manage. Finally, the lack of representation for the Row Offices was a glaring omission as they struggled to have their interests heard in the review process.

The second recommended amendment was my desire to reduce the back-and-forth political tugs of war waged through the Charter. The Charter should be a stable document that does not ebb and flow with rapid changes in the political winds. At the time, a couple of issues, such as the UOPP and the direct election of Row Offices, should not be changed through the Charter on an annual basis.

*Proposed Amendment 1*

The intent of the following amendment is threefold. First, the amendment reduces the number of Review Committee members from 27 to 18, which is a better working size. Second, the amendment provides the Row Offices representation on the Review Committee by creating a Selection Committee. Finally, a non-voting (except for ties) chairperson is created to preside over the Committee. Bold underline font indicates text added, and strikethrough font indicates text removed.

**Sec. 9.05 (D)**

On or before March 1, 1996, and on or before January 1 of each eight (8) years thereafter, there shall be constituted a Charter Review Committee for the purpose of reviewing this Charter and determining the desirability of amendment(s) thereto. The Charter Review Committee shall be composed of **eighteen (18) voting** ~~twenty-seven (27)~~ members **and one (1) chairperson who only votes to break ties. The voting members shall be** ~~with~~ one (1) member of the Commission from each Commission district to be nominated by the Knox County Commission and nine (9) citizen members who are registered voters of Knox County and who are not members of the Commission to be nominated by ~~the~~ **a Charter Selection Committee. The Charter Selection Committee shall consist of two (2) Commissioners, the Mayor, the Sheriff, the Trustee, the Register of Deeds, the County Clerk, the Law Director and the Property Assessor. Charter Selection Committee members shall not serve on the Charter Review Committee. The Charter Selection Committee shall also select the chairperson who shall be a registered voter of Knox County and who is not a member of Commission and nor a member of the Charter Selection Committee.** ~~Knox County Commission and nine (9) citizen members who are registered voters of Knox County who are not members of the Commission to be nominated by the Knox County Mayor.~~ Not more **than one (1)** ~~two (2) such~~ citizen **voting members** ~~who are registered voters of Knox County~~ shall be nominated from each Commission district. Each nominee shall be voted upon individually by the **Charter Selection Committee** ~~Knox County Commission~~. In the event a nominee does not receive a majority of votes, then the

> person who nominated said nominee shall bring forth a different nominee. It shall be the duty of the Charter Review Committee to give ample opportunity to County officeholders and members of the general public to make suggested changes to this Charter. In accordance with state law, the Charter Review **Committee** ~~commission~~ shall either: (1) certify to the Knox County Election Commission such amendment(s) which it has determined to be desirable; or (2) certify to the **Charter Selection Committee** ~~Mayor~~ and to the County Commission a statement that it does not recommend amending this Charter. **The Charter Review Committee shall disband on or before the second Tuesday of November in the same year the Committee was constituted.**

Figure 3. My first proposed amendment. Not accepted.

## Proposed Amendment 2

The amendment intends to allow time to pass before a proposed amendment can appear before the voters again to reduce voter fatigue issues. Bold underline font indicates text added, and strikethrough font indicates text removed.

> **Sec. 9.05 (F)**
> **No proposed charter amendment or a substantially similar proposed amendment to be submitted to the voters of Knox County shall have previously appeared on a ballot before the voters of the County during any preceding five (5) years.**

Figure 4. My second proposed amendment. Not accepted.

## Knox County Charter

I relied on this version of the Knox County Charter and online links for reference throughout the Charter Review process. I kept this file on my computer for reference on an as-needed basis. I cannot attest to the accuracy or correctness of this document.

## PART I - CHARTER

We, the people of Knox County, Tennessee, in order to establish the structure and to enlarge the powers of our County Government, to insure that it is just, orderly, efficient and fully responsible to the people, and to secure the benefit of home rule and self-government for Knox County to the fullest extent possible under the Constitution of the State of Tennessee, do hereby publish, declare and adopt this Charter of Knox County, Tennessee, as the fundamental law for the government of this County.

    ARTICLE I. - POWERS AND FUNCTIONS
    ARTICLE II. - LEGISLATIVE BRANCH
    ARTICLE III. - EXECUTIVE BRANCH
    ARTICLE IV. - OTHER OFFICERS
    ARTICLE V. - JUDICIAL BRANCH
    ARTICLE VI. - EDUCATION
    ARTICLE VII. - PENSIONS
    ARTICLE VIII. - ELECTIONS
    ARTICLE IX. - GENERAL PROVISIONS
    ARTICLE X. - TRANSITION PROVISIONS

### ARTICLE I. - POWERS AND FUNCTIONS

    Sec. 1.01. - Powers and functions.
    Sec. 1.02. - Private and local affairs.
    Sec. 1.03. - Public corporation powers.
    Sec. 1.04. - Public corporation rights.
    Sec. 1.05. - Rights reserved to the people.

**Sec. 1.01. - Powers and functions.**

The Knox County Government shall exercise any power or perform any function which is not denied by the Constitution of the State of Tennessee. It is the intent of this Charter that limitations on the powers of County Government shall be strictly construed, and that grants of power to County Government shall be liberally construed.

Sec. 1.02. - Private and local affairs.

With regard to private and local affairs, all lawful powers are vested in the Executive of Knox County and the Commission of Knox County, except those powers reserved to the judiciary. This investment of legislative, executive and other powers and duties shall be as full and complete, and the authority to perform or to direct them as broad, as is possible to delegate or confer, it being the intent to invest in the government of Knox County every authority, power and responsibility for the conduct of the affairs of the government of Knox County, including the powers to adopt and enforce resolutions, ordinances and emergency ordinances.

Sec. 1.03. - Public corporation powers.

The government described herein shall be a public corporation vested with any and all powers which counties are, or may hereafter be, authorized or required to exercise under the Constitution and all applicable laws of the State of Tennessee, including, but not limited to, the power to do all things necessary or convenient for the provision of public services or public works projects now or hereafter authorized or contemplated by the Constitution and all applicable laws of the State of Tennessee.

Sec. 1.04. - Public corporation rights.

The government of Knox County shall be a public corporation, with the right of perpetual succession, capable of suing and being sued, capable of purchasing, receiving and holding real and personal property and of selling, leasing, or disposing of the same to the fullest extent permitted, and having all express, implied and inferred rights necessary or convenient to the exercise of its public corporation powers.

Sec. 1.05. - Rights reserved to the people.

No provisions of this Charter, and no action by any officer or employee of the County acting under its authority, shall infringe upon rights, privileges and powers now or hereafter reserved or guaranteed to individual persons or to the people by the Constitution of the United States of America or the Constitution of the State of Tennessee.

## ARTICLE II. - LEGISLATIVE BRANCH

Sec. 2.01. - Legislative powers.
Sec. 2.02. - Other powers.
Sec. 2.03. - Membership and election; district, seats, reapportionment and redistricting.
Sec. 2.04. - Commission members' salary and compensation.
Sec. 2.05. - Meetings and quorum.
Sec. 2.06. - Election of chairman(woman) and vice chairman(woman).
Sec. 2.07. - Removal of member of the Commission.
Sec. 2.08. - Vacancy.
Sec. 2.09. - Ordinances, emergency ordinances and resolutions.
Sec. 2.10. - Signature and veto by the Mayor of Knox County.

### Sec. 2.01. - Legislative powers.

The legislative power of the County is vested in the Commission of Knox County (hereinafter referred to as the "Commission"), which is the Legislative Branch and Legislative Body of Knox County. The legislative power of the County includes all lawful authority to adopt ordinances, emergency ordinances and resolutions governing the operation of government or regulating the conduct and affairs of the residents of the County, to adopt and amend the County budget, to fix all County tax rates and to provide for the collection of all County taxes, to release County taxpayers from double taxes, when such has occurred, to provide for corrections in tax lists, to appropriate County funds for any and all lawful purposes, and to exercise all other authority of a legislative nature which is vested in the County by the Constitution and all applicable laws of the State of Tennessee. The Commission may adopt any ordinance, emergency ordinance or resolution which is not in conflict with the Constitution or general laws of the State of Tennessee or this Charter.

### Sec. 2.02. - Other powers.

A. The Commission is vested with all other powers of the government of Knox County not specifically, or by necessary implication, vested in some other official of the County by the Constitution of the State of Tennessee, by this Charter or by law not inconsistent with this Charter. However, neither the Commission nor the Chairman(woman) of the Commission shall exercise any powers or perform any functions of the County Government which are vested, by the terms of this Charter, in either the Executive Branch or the Judicial Branch. Whenever any statute of the State of Tennessee purports to authorize the monthly or quarterly county court (or county chairman[(woman)] or county judge), the county commission (or chairman[(woman)] of the county commission) or the county executive to perform any administrative or executive act or function, then such act or function shall be performed by the Executive of Knox County except as otherwise provided in this Charter.

B. The Commission shall provide annually, by resolution, for an independent audit of the accounts and other evidences of financial transactions of the County and of every County office and such other special audits as the Commission deems necessary. Such audits shall be made by a certified public accountant or by a firm of certified public accountants designated by the Commission, and no individual auditor or member of an auditing firm so designated shall have any personal financial interest, direct or indirect, in the fiscal affairs of the County or of any of its offices. The designated certified public accountants shall be qualified by training and experience and shall have sufficient staff to perform the audits. No individual certified public accountant or firm of certified public accountants shall be employed to perform the audits for more than four (4) successive years.

C. By ordinance, the Commission shall establish rules and regulations governing all County purchases, sales, contracts for services and disposal of surplus property.

D. No sale or transfer of real property, or any interests therein, owned by the County shall be valid unless approved by resolution of the Commission.

E. By resolution which shall not be subject to veto by the Executive of Knox County, the Commission shall have the power to authorize the borrowing of money and the issuance of bonds, notes and other evidences of indebtedness of the County and all matters pertaining thereto. Such a resolution shall be effective immediately upon its adoption by the Commission.

F. By resolution, the Commission may employ, contract with, or otherwise hire, any person(s) or business entity(ies) which it deems necessary to the exercise of the powers vested in it unless otherwise provided by this Charter.

G. By ordinance, the Commission may establish and name such special districts and, in connection therewith, shall provide for assessments, levies and collections of taxes and assessments with respect to any or all property, real or personal, or privileges within any such district and the pledge of the revenues derived and to be derived therefrom, all as in its judgment may be necessary or appropriate for the exercise within such district of any one or more of the public corporation rights or powers of the government of Knox County not then being exercised for the benefit of all citizens of the County. The subsequent exercise of any such right or power for the benefit of all citizens of the County shall not impair any special district theretofore established or any contracts, pledges or obligations of the government of Knox County with respect thereto.

H. Upon adoption of an approving resolution in each instance by the affirmative vote of two-thirds (2/3) of the entire Commission, the Commission and its authorized committees shall have full power and authority to hold public hearings, with power to subpoena witnesses and to administer oaths where necessary or desirable, for the purpose of either (1) gathering information necessary or desirable for the purpose of considering proposed Commission legislation, or (2) investigating any allegation of violations of this Charter, ordinances or emergency ordinances of the Commission brought by either the Executive of Knox County or any member of the Commission against any elected official or employee of the County. No such hearing shall be held with or without such subpoena power having been exercised except when a quorum of the Commission or any authorized committee, as appropriate, is present.

I. By resolution, the Commission may appoint members of the following boards and commissions: Knox County Board of Adjustments and Enforcement; Knox County Agricultural Extension Committee; Knox County Air Pollution Control Board; Knox County Ambulance Review Commission; Knox County Board of Construction Standards and Applications; Knox County Board of Equalization; Knox County Board of Health; Knox County Housing Authority; Knox County Jail Inspection Committee; Knox County Library Board of Trustees; The Public Building Authority of the County of Knox and the City of Knoxville, Tennessee; Knox County Old Records Commission; Knox County Sheriff's Department Merit System Council; and two members of Knox County Personnel Board. All such appointees shall be residents of Knox County at the time of their appointment and at all times while serving on said board or commission. The Commission shall have the authority, by resolution, to remove and discharge all such members for good cause shown.

(Ref. of 8-1-96)

**Sec. 2.03. - Membership and election; district, seats, reapportionment and redistricting.**

A. The Commission members shall be elected by the people of Knox County in the following manner:

(1) The Commission under this Charter shall consist of nine (9) members elected from nine (9) districts, and two (2) members elected at-large through County-wide vote. The nine (9) members elected by districts shall be residents of and represent the districts from which they are elected. Any resident of any such district desiring to stand for election to the Commission as a district representative and qualified to do so pursuant to the requirements of this Charter shall qualify in accordance with applicable law for the specific seat representing such Commission district. The nine (9) district seats shall be referred to as Commission Seats one (1) through nine (9) respectively with the numbers corresponding to the district numbers from which the district Commissioners are elected. Any resident of Knox County desiring to stand for election to Commission as an at-large representative and qualified to do so pursuant to the requirements of this Charter shall qualify in accordance with applicable law for one (1) of the specific at-large seats elected through County-wide vote. The two (2) at-large seats shall be referred to as Commission Seats ten (10) and eleven (11). Any qualified voter in any Commission District may vote for one (1) candidate for each Commission seat representing such District, one (1) candidate for at-large Commission Seat ten (10) and one (1) candidate for at-large Commission Seat eleven (11).

(2) The regular terms of Commission members shall be four (4) years. Commission Seats 1, 2, 4, 5, 6, 8, and 9 shall be elected in the County primary and general election of 2010 for an initial extended term of six (6) years and every four (4) years thereafter. Commission Seats 3, 7, 10, and 11 shall be elected in the County primary and general election of 2010 and every four (4) years thereafter.

(3) The foregoing provisions of Sections 2.03.A(1) and (2) shall become effective September 1, 2010 and prior thereto to the extent necessary to permit primary and general elections to be held for the eleven Commission Seats, to take office effective September 1, 2010.

Personal Notes and Position Papers

B. On or before December 31, 1991, and every ten (10) years thereafter, it shall be the duty of the Commission, based upon the most recent Federal decennial census, to reapportion and/or redistrict the Commission seats so as to comply with constitutional requirements. The voting precincts of Knox County shall be established by the Commission by ordinance unless otherwise provided by applicable law.

C. No person shall be eligible to serve as a member of the Commission unless that person shall have attained the age of eighteen (18) and is a resident of, and a registered voter in, the district from which such person seeks election on the date he/she filed his/her nominating petition and has been a resident of both the County and the district for one (1) year prior to such person's election; provided, however, that the district residency requirement shall not apply in the first general election at which Commission seats appear on the ballot following any reapportionment or redistricting of Commission districts. A member of the Commission shall remain a resident of the Commission district which such member represents during his/her term of office.

Note—See editor's note at the end of this section.

D. The Commission shall adopt its own rules of order and procedure. All resolutions, ordinances and emergency ordinances shall be adopted in accordance with the Constitution, all applicable laws of the State of Tennessee and this Charter.

E. In all proceedings of the Commission to either elect officers of the Commission or to fill vacancies in elective offices, the following procedure shall be followed:

(1) Nominations may be made by members of the Commission only.

(2) Each member of the Commission may vote in favor of one (1) nominee, by name, only.

(3) Election of a nominee shall require a majority vote of the membership of the Commission. Prior to such election, the Commission shall, by resolution or ordinance, establish the procedure for arriving at a majority vote.

F. When any public office is to be filled by the Commission, if any member of the Commission accepts the nomination as a candidate for such public office, the following procedure shall be followed:

(1) No member of the Commission who is absent from any proceeding to fill a public office shall be eligible to have his/her name placed in nomination unless either the Chairman(woman) of the Commission or the County Clerk shall have present at such meeting of the Commission a written acceptance of such nomination signed by such member of the Commission.

(2) If a Commission member's name is placed in nomination, the Chairman(woman) of the Commission shall, prior to the first vote, require that member to either accept or decline the nomination. A refusal to either accept or decline shall disqualify that member for nomination.

(3) No vote shall be recorded in favor of any member of the Commission who has either declined nomination or has been otherwise disqualified.

(4) The acceptance of nomination by a member of the Commission shall automatically disqualify such member to vote to fill that office.

(5) If the Commission member is elected, his/her seat on the Commission shall immediately be vacant.

(Ref. of 11-4-08)

> Editor's note— Pursuant to T.C.A. § 2-5-151 and Section 9.05.C of the Knox County Charter, the voters of Knox County voted on November 4, 2008 to amend the Knox County Charter by adding a new sentence to the end of Section 2.03.C, (scheduled to take effect on September 1, 2010) that reads: "Further, no person shall be eligible to serve as a member of the Commission who is employed in any other position by Knox County." This Amendment was challenged in Knox County Chancery Court in the Case of *Drew, et al. v. Knox County, Case No. 176120-1*. On April 16, 2010, the Court invalidated the above-quoted sentence. Unless or until that matter is appealed, the new sentence added to the end of Section 2.03.C is not included in, nor a part of, the Knox County Charter and Section 9.08.C shall remain in full force and effect.

**Sec. 2.04. - Commission members' salary and compensation.**

The Commission shall set the compensation for members of the Commission which shall not be less than One Thousand Dollars ($1,000.00) per month. The compensation allowed any member of the Commission shall not be decreased during the term of office and shall not be increased more than thirty percent (30%) during the term of office. Any increase in compensation shall be set by the annual budget.

Personal Notes and Position Papers

**Sec. 2.05. - Meetings and quorum.**

The Commission shall meet at least once each month at a time and place to be determined by the Commission. A quorum for the purpose of conducting business shall be a majority of the membership of the Commission.

**Sec. 2.06. - Election of chairman(woman) and vice chairman(woman).**

The Commission, at its first session on or after September 1, 1990, and annually thereafter, shall elect from its membership a chairman(woman), vice chairman(woman), and such other officers as the Commission deems necessary. The election procedures shall follow those established pursuant to Section 2.03E.

**Sec. 2.07. - Removal of member of the Commission.**

A member of the Commission may be removed from office according to the laws of the State of Tennessee.

**Sec. 2.08. - Vacancy.**

If a vacancy occurs on the Board of County Commissioners due to death, resignation, removal, or disability, the vacancy shall be filled by the Commission with a person meeting the qualifications for said position until his/her successor is elected in the next general election and sworn; provided, however, if such vacancy occurs within sixty (60) days prior to the next general election, the person so selected by the Commission to fill the vacancy shall serve the remainder of the term of that Commission seat. Said selection shall not occur until such time as the Commission conducts a duly noticed public hearing during which time interested, qualified candidates will be interviewed by the Commission.

(Ref. of 8-5-10)

**Sec. 2.09. - Ordinances, emergency ordinances and resolutions.**

A. *Generally.*

    (1) The Commission shall exercise its legislative authority by resolution, ordinance, or emergency ordinance as hereinafter set forth.

    (2) No ordinance, emergency ordinance or resolution shall become effective which embraces more than one (1)

subject, the subject to be expressed in its caption.

(3) All ordinances, emergency ordinances, and resolutions which repeal, revise or amend former ordinances, emergency ordinances or resolutions shall recite in their caption the number and date of adoption of the ordinance, emergency ordinance or resolution repealed, revised or amended.

(4) In order to become effective, any ordinance or resolution shall receive a majority vote of the membership of the Commission except the following:

> (a) Any ordinance proposing an amendment to this Charter shall be adopted by a favorable vote of two-thirds (2/3) of the membership of the Commission.
>
> (b) Any resolution authorizing the Commission, or its authorized committee(s), to hold public hearings pursuant to Section 2.02.H of this Charter shall be adopted by a favorable vote of two-thirds (2/3) of the membership of the Commission.
>
> (c) Any ordinance pursuant to Section 2.03.A.(2) of this Charter shall be adopted by a favorable vote of two-thirds (2/3) of the membership of the Commission.
>
> (d) All emergency ordinances shall be adopted in accordance with applicable law and this Charter.

(5) No ordinance, emergency ordinance or resolution shall become effective unless the following procedure is followed:

> (a) Each member of the Commission present shall distinctly, audibly or visually cast his/her vote, and the County Clerk shall record, in writing, each member's vote as "aye," "nay," or "abstain."
>
> (b) At the conclusion of each vote, either the Chairman(woman) of the Commission or the County Clerk shall distinctly and audibly announce the tally of each category of votes cast.
>
> (c) No member of the Commission shall change his/her vote after the vote is announced unless

granted the right to do so by a majority of the membership of the Commission at such Commission meeting at which the original vote was cast. It shall be the duty of the Chairman(woman) of the Commission or the County Clerk, at the time of such vote change, to announce distinctly, audibly or visually the caption of the subject legislation as well as the name and manner of vote change of such member of the Commission.

(d) Upon the adjournment of each and every meeting of the Commission, it shall be the duty of the County Clerk to maintain and preserve, unchanged, as public records available for inspection during reasonable office hours, the voting record for each and every ordinance, emergency ordinance and resolution.

(6) It shall be the duty of the County Clerk to deliver to the Executive of Knox County true and attested copies of all ordinances, emergency ordinances and resolutions within four (4) days of final adoption by the Commission.

(7) It shall be the duty of the County Clerk to deliver to the County Law Director true and attested copies of all ordinances, emergency ordinances and resolutions within thirty (30) days of their effective date.

(8) The County Clerk shall number and compile in an ordinance book all ordinances and emergency ordinances and shall number and compile in a resolution book all resolutions and shall preserve such books in the County Clerk's office. The County Clerk shall furnish a true copy for a reasonable fee to any person so requesting.

(9) It shall be the duty of the County Clerk to provide copies of this Charter and amendments thereto, together with all ordinances and emergency ordinances, to the Knox County Code Commission as provided in Section 4.05 of this Charter.

(10) The County Clerk may delegate to his/her deputy(ies) any or all duties imposed upon the County Clerk by this Charter; provided, however, nothing in this Paragraph (10) shall be construed to relieve the County Clerk of any and all responsibilities imposed upon him/her by this Charter.

B.   *Ordinances.*

   (1)   An ordinance shall be considered to be on the agenda of any meeting of the Commission only if:

   (a)   the caption of such ordinance is quoted verbatim in the agenda for such meeting and a copy of such agenda has been made available to each and every member of the Commission not later than five (5) days prior to such Commission meeting; and

   (b)   a copy of such ordinance has been made available to each member of the Commission at least forty-eight (48) hours prior to such meeting.

   (2)   To become effective, each ordinance shall be adopted in accordance with all applicable laws of the State of Tennessee; provided, however, in the absence of any applicable law in conflict with this Charter, to become effective, each ordinance shall be approved by a majority of the members of the Commission upon two (2) readings.

   (3)   An ordinance shall take effect on the fifteenth (15th) day following its passage on final reading.

   (4)   Ordinances imposing fines or imprisonment as punishment for violation thereof shall be enforced by the Chief Law Enforcement Officer of the County unless such ordinance otherwise provides. Persons charged with violation of such an ordinance shall be tried in the Court of General Sessions. Any fines or penalties, or both, and court costs collected for such violation, shall be paid into the County general fund.

C.   *Emergency ordinances.*

   (1)   An emergency ordinance shall be so designated in its caption.

   (2)   To become effective, an emergency ordinance shall be adopted in accordance with all applicable laws of the State of Tennessee; provided, however, that in the absence of applicable law in conflict with this Charter, an emergency ordinance shall be adopted by an affirmative vote of two-thirds (2/3) of the members of the Commission pursuant to the following procedure:

(a) An emergency ordinance which appears on the regular agenda, as any other ordinance, pursuant to Section 2.09.B, shall take effect either upon the signature of the Executive of Knox County or, in the absence of a veto as hereinafter provided and without the signature of the Executive of Knox County, upon the eighth (8th) day following its adoption upon one (1) reading by the Commission, whichever first occurs.

(b) An emergency ordinance may be added to the agenda of any meeting of the Commission at which a quorum is present by unanimous consent of the members of the Commission present and voting for the sole purpose of a reading thereof; such emergency ordinance may be adopted upon second (2nd) reading at the next meeting of the Commission. Such emergency ordinance shall become effective either upon the signature of the Executive of Knox County or, in the absence of a veto as hereinafter provided and without the signature of the Executive of Knox County, upon the eighth (8th) day following its adoption, whichever first occurs.

D. *Resolutions.* All resolutions shall be adopted upon receiving a majority vote of the membership of the Commission upon one (1) reading and shall become effective in accordance with Section 2.10 of this Charter.

**Sec. 2.10. - Signature and veto by the Mayor of Knox County.**

A. Every ordinance, emergency ordinance and resolution shall be submitted to the Mayor of Knox County for approval or veto; provided, however, that this requirement shall not apply to (1) resolutions authorizing the borrowing of money and the issuance of bonds and notes and other evidences of indebtedness of the County and all matters pertaining thereto, as provided in Section 2.02.E of this Charter, which resolutions shall become effective immediately upon their adoption by the Commission, or (2) ordinances, emergency ordinances and resolutions affecting zoning regulations, which shall become effective immediately upon their adoption by the Commission. Upon the signature of the Mayor of Knox County, an ordinance, emergency ordinance or resolution becomes effective as provided in Sections 2.09 and 2.10 of this Charter.

B. Any ordinance or resolution vetoed by the Mayor of Knox County shall be returned to the County Clerk within ten (10) days after the ordinance or resolution is required by this Charter to be submitted to the Mayor. Any emergency ordinance vetoed by the Mayor of Knox County shall be returned to the County Clerk within three (3) days after the emergency ordinance is required by this Charter to be submitted to the Mayor. The County Clerk shall notify the members of the Commission, in writing, within five (5) days of receipt by the County Clerk.

C. Any vote of the Commission to override the veto of the Mayor of Knox County shall be taken within thirty-five (35) days of the expiration of the period required of the County Clerk to notify the members of the Commission of the veto which is the subject of such override vote. The affirmative vote of not less than a majority plus one (1) of the membership of the Commission shall be required to override the veto of the Mayor of Knox County; provided, however, in the case of ordinances and emergency ordinances requiring a two-thirds (2/3) vote for original passage, a two-thirds (2/3) vote of the membership of the Commission shall be required to override the veto of the Mayor of Knox County. The ordinance, emergency ordinance or resolution shall immediately become effective upon the Commission overriding the veto.

D. If the Mayor of Knox County fails either to sign or veto an ordinance or resolution and to report this action to the County Clerk within ten (10) days after the ordinance or resolution is required by this Charter to be submitted to the Mayor (or within three (3) days in the case of an emergency ordinance), the Mayor of Knox County shall have no further power to veto the ordinance, emergency ordinance or resolution, and it shall become effective without the signature of the Mayor of Knox County upon the expiration of the time periods in this paragraph provided, or at a later date if the ordinance or resolution so provides.

(Ref. of 8-6-04)

## ARTICLE III. - EXECUTIVE BRANCH

Sec. 3.01. - Executive and administrative powers.
Sec. 3.02. - Executive branch.
Sec. 3.03. - The Mayor's duties.
Sec. 3.04. - Mayor—Term, qualifications, compensation.
Sec. 3.05. - Same—Vacancy.
Sec. 3.06. - County departments and other entities.
Sec. 3.07. - Budget procedures.
Sec. 3.08. - Knox County Law Director.
Sec. 3.09. - Reserved.
Sec. 3.10. - Knox County Code Commission.

### Sec. 3.01. - Executive and administrative powers.

The executive and administrative powers of the Knox County Government shall be vested in, and exercised by, the Mayor of Knox County (hereinafter referred to as the "Mayor"), also called the Executive Branch, and, under the Mayor's control and direction, by such subordinate major divisions, departments, boards, offices, officers and agencies as established from time to time.

(Ref. of 8-6-04)

### Sec. 3.02. - Executive branch.

The Mayor shall be the head of the Executive Branch of Knox County Government, responsible for the exercising of all executive and administrative functions of the County Government and shall be the chief fiscal officer of the County. The Mayor shall devote his full time to the performance of his duties as the Mayor.

(Ref. of 8-6-04)

### Sec. 3.03. - The Mayor's duties.

The Mayor shall:

> A. See that all provisions of this Charter, resolutions, ordinances and emergency ordinances of the Commission and all applicable laws of the State of Tennessee subject to execution by Knox County are faithfully executed; provided, however, the Mayor shall not assume any of the constitutional, statutory or Charter duties of the Sheriff.
>
> B. Prepare and submit to the Commission, with the assistance of appropriate department heads and other

responsible officials, budgets and financial reports. The Mayor shall present a consolidated budget of the County to the Commission on or before June 1 of each and every year in order for the Commission either to approve said budget as presented or to modify and amend the same as may be deemed requisite in order to determine the amount of taxes necessary to be levied. The adoption of the budget by the Commission shall be by resolution.

C. Examine regularly the accounts, records and operations of every department, office and agency of the County; make regular reports to the Commission on the affairs of the County; keep the Commission fully advised of the financial condition and the future needs of the County; and make such recommendations to the Commission on County affairs as he/she deems appropriate.

D. Take such other executive and administrative actions as are permitted or required by this Charter and all applicable laws of the State of Tennessee or as may be prescribed by the Commission.

E. Have power to contract with various municipalities, other governmental units or public corporations in the County for the consolidation of services and functions, upon the authorization of the Commission by resolution. The Mayor may also contract with one or more states or counties, or both, for institutional or other services which may be rendered more efficiently or economically.

F. Provide for and maintain all accounting systems necessary for the County and for each department, office and agency thereof. The Mayor shall maintain such systems in accordance with generally accepted accounting principles applicable to governmental entities, keeping accounting records for, and exercising financial and budgeting control over, such department, office or agency. All warrants in payment of obligations of the County shall be signed by the Mayor, either in person or by facsimile, except where another officer is authorized so to do by either applicable law or this Charter.

G. Have veto power over the annual budgets of the County which may be exercised by vetoing specific items or parts of items without invalidating the whole. The veto shall be exercised and may be overridden by the procedure as provided in Section 2.10 of this Charter; provided, however, that no veto pursuant to this paragraph shall be valid unless the Mayor, within the time provided for vetoes in Section 2.10.B of this Charter, shall provide, in writing to the County Clerk, the following information:

(1) a list of the specific items, or parts of items, vetoed; and

(2) an amount for each specific item, or parts of items, less than, and in lieu of, the amount contained in each specific item, or parts of items, vetoed; and

(3) an explanation by the Mayor as to his/her reason for each such veto.

Such reduced amount of each specific item, or parts of items, shall become a part of such annual budget if such item, or parts of items, are not overridden by the Commission; provided, however, nothing contained in this paragraph shall be construed as prohibiting the Commission thereafter, by resolution pursuant to Sections 2.09 and 2.10, amending or supplementing such annual budget, including such vetoed items.

H. Appoint members of all boards, authorities and commissions not delegated by this Charter to appointment by the Commission. All appointees shall be residents of Knox County at the time of their appointment and at all times while serving on said board, authority or commission. Such members may be removed and discharged for good cause shown.

I. Have the right to serve, individually, or to appoint from administrative assistants, executive assistants or any head of any division or department of the County, in writing, a designee, to serve in place and stead of the Mayor on any board or commission of which the Mayor is a member by law. Said designee shall have all powers, including the power to vote, as are conferred upon the Mayor. Any designee appointed by the Mayor under the provisions of this Section shall be appointed to serve in that capacity for at least one (1) year, or for the remainder of the term of office of the Mayor, whichever is less. During such periods of appointments, either the specified designee or the Mayor may exercise the voting powers granted by this Section. However, at any meeting attended by the Mayor, only the Mayor shall exercise the voting power.

J.  Negotiate and execute loans, bonds, notes and other evidences of indebtedness of the County to the extent provided in the resolution authorizing the same.

K.  Maintain the records of County indebtedness and have charge of the payment of principal and interest thereon.

L.  Examine all contracts, orders and other documents by which financial obligations are incurred by the County, or by any of its officials or officers, and indicate the availability of funds to meet these obligations, and certify thereto.

M.  Have the sole power and authority to enter into contracts on behalf of Knox County, except as otherwise provided in this Charter. Contracts and purchases on behalf of the County shall be entered into by the Mayor or the Mayor's designee. On all contracts in an amount greater than $50,000, or such greater amount as established in advance by the Commission, the Mayor shall obtain the approval of the Commission by resolution prior to execution.

N.  Develop purchasing regulations for all purchases made with funds that have been collected for the use of Knox County. Any such purchasing regulations shall be enacted as an Ordinance by the Knox County Commission. To the maximum extent allowed by law, each constitutional, statutory or Charter official of Knox County, whether appointed or elected, shall be required to follow the provisions of the Knox County Purchasing Ordinance for construction or purchases of goods and services with public funds.

(Ref. of 8-6-04)

### Sec. 3.04. - Mayor—Term, qualifications, compensation.

The Mayor shall be elected by the qualified voters of Knox County each four (4) years, commencing with the 1990 County general election, and shall take office on September 1 following his/her election. The Mayor shall be twenty-five (25) years of age or older, a resident of Knox County at least one (1) year prior to filing for this office and shall remain a resident of Knox County during his/her term of office. The Mayor's compensation shall be set by the Commission which compensation shall be greater than the compensation paid any other elected County official. Such compensation shall be paid in equal monthly installments. The salary of the Mayor may be changed from time to time by resolution of the Commission; provided, however, that such compensation shall not be decreased during the term for which the Mayor was elected; and, provided further, the Commission shall take no action changing the Mayor's salary for any succeeding term of the Mayor during the year in which the Mayor is to be elected.

(Ref. of 8-6-04)

**Sec. 3.05. - Same—Vacancy.**

If a vacancy occurs in the office of Mayor by death, resignation, removal, or disability, the vacancy shall be filled by the Commission with a person meeting the qualifications for said position until his/her successor is elected in the next general election and sworn; provided, however, if such vacancy occurs within sixty (60) days prior to the next general election, the person so selected by the Commission to fill the vacancy shall serve the remainder of the term of the Mayor. Said selection shall not occur until such time as the Commission conducts a duly noticed public hearing during which time interested, qualified candidates will be interviewed by the Commission.

(Ref. of 8-6-04; Ref. of 8-5-10)

**Sec. 3.06. - County departments and other entities.**

A. The Mayor, subject to approval by resolution of the Commission, may create or abolish major departments of County Government with each department having a Department Director. The Department Directors of the County shall be appointed by the Mayor, shall be subject to dismissal by the Mayor without cause, and shall be residents of Knox County at the time they assume the duties of their office and at all other times while serving the County in such capacity.

B. The duties, powers and functions of the departments of the County Government shall be generally as set by ordinance, and their jurisdiction shall extend throughout the County Government.

C. The Mayor, subject to approval or ratification by resolution of the Commission, may create and establish, or cause the creation and establishment of, nonprofit corporations or authorities in accordance with general law to act for or on behalf of the County alone or in conjunction with one or more municipalities, counties, other governmental units, public corporations, or combination thereof, for public, civic or charitable purposes. Any such corporation shall have all the powers and privileges provided by general law unless restricted by its corporate charter. No County funds shall be appropriated, contributed or loaned to any such corporation nor shall the County enter into any contract with such corporation without the prior approval of the Commission by resolution.

(Ref. of 8-6-04)

**Sec. 3.07. - Budget procedures.**

A.   The head of each County department or County office, including constitutional officers, shall, upon request, furnish to the Mayor in a form specified by the Mayor:

> (1)   estimates of the revenues and expenditures of the department or office for the ensuing fiscal year and/or balance of the current fiscal year,
>
> (2)   estimates of the costs of any capital improvements pending or proposed to be undertaken (i) within the ensuing fiscal year and (ii) within the four (4) fiscal years immediately thereafter, and
>
> (3)   such other information as the Mayor requests.

B.   All constitutional officers shall submit their budgets to the Mayor no later than May 1 of each and every year. The Mayor shall submit a consolidated budget to the Commission.

C.   All offices or departments which receive appropriations from County Government shall utilize such appropriations strictly in accordance with the applicable provisions of the budget as finally approved or amended; provided, however, upon the recommendation of the chief elected administrative officer of the unit or department, or if none, the Mayor, the Commission may provide for approval of transfers between line items within the budget of offices or departments. The chief elected administrative officer of the unit or department, or if none, the Mayor, shall affirmatively certify that such transfer will not impair the necessary functions or operations of the office(s) or department(s). Capital appropriations shall not be altered or varied except with the approval of the Commission by resolution. No appropriation shall be reduced below the level required either by law or by bond covenants.

(Ref. of 8-6-04)

### Sec. 3.08. - Knox County Law Director.

A.  The office of County Law Director is hereby established. The Law Director shall be an attorney duly licensed to practice law in the State of Tennessee, shall devote full time to the duties of the office of Law Director and shall not engage in the private practice of law while holding the office of Law Director for Knox County except for the purpose of disposing of matters or cases for which he/she was employed as of the date of his/her election.

B.  The salary of said Law Director is hereby fixed as the same salary as is provided by law for judges of the Circuit and Chancery courts for the State of Tennessee, which salary shall not be lowered during the Law Director's term of office. The Law Director's salary shall be payable in equal monthly installments from the general funds of the County.

C.  The Law Director shall be elected by the qualified voters of Knox County at the 1992 County general election and at the County general election at which the Assessor of Property is elected and each and every four (4) years thereafter. The Knox County Law Director shall be subject to the term limits provisions of this Charter to the same extent as any Constitutional officer of Knox County Government, as that term is defined by Article VII, Section 1 of the Tennessee Constitution.

D.  It shall be the duty of the Law Director to take the oath of office prescribed for other County officials and appropriate to his/her office before entering upon the discharge of his/her duties, and thereafter to execute and administer all of the legal affairs of the County, including litigation, drafting of contracts or other documents, instruments and papers, the investigation of titles, and to advise and counsel County officials and the Commission on all legal matters affecting their respective offices. No elected or appointed officer or employee of the County shall employ any other attorney to represent the County or any officer, board, or member of the Commission unless he/she shall first be authorized and empowered to do so by resolution of the Commission. Provided, however, that the Law Director shall have authority, within the budget approved by the County Commission for this purpose, to hire outside counsel when, in the judgment of the Law Director, such is necessary for the fulfillment of his/her duties under the Section.

E.  The County shall pay all reasonable and necessary expenses incurred by the Law Director in the discharge of his official duties, subject to submission of such bills, receipts, invoices, or other documents and papers as may be required by the accounting practices established for the County Government.

F. The Law Director is hereby authorized to employ such assistants and office personnel as may be necessary for the discharge of the Law Director's duties at salaries to be set by the Commission. The Commission shall provide suitable offices, appurtenances, and conveniences for the Law Director and the use of his/her assistants and office personnel. The Commission shall also furnish the Law Director with appropriate equipment, furniture, and supplies as may be necessary in the performance of his/her duties, including an appropriate law library.

G. If a vacancy occurs in the office of Law Director by death, resignation, removal, or disability, the vacancy shall be filled by the Commission with a person meeting the qualifications for said position, as provided in Section 3.08.A, until his/her successor is elected in the next general election and sworn; provided, however, if such vacancy occurs within sixty (60) days prior to the next general election, the person so selected by the Commission to fill the vacancy shall serve the remainder of the term of the Law Director upon the conclusion of a duly noticed public hearing during which time interested, qualified candidates will be interviewed by the Commission.

(Ref. of 8-6-04; Ref. of 8-5-10)

Sec. 3.09. - Reserved.

> Editor's note— The referendum of November 7, 2006, repealed § 3.09 in its entirety, which pertained to the position of sheriff and derived from original codification. For current provisions relating to the position of sheriff, the user's attention is directed to section 4.02 of this Charter.

Sec. 3.10. - Knox County Code Commission.

A. There is hereby created the Knox County Code Commission, which shall be composed of the County Mayor, the County Clerk, and three members of the Knox County Commission, and which, for budgetary purposes, shall be treated as a department of the County Government. The County Commission shall appoint the County Commission members of the Code Commission. The members shall be selected upon this section becoming a law, and shall serve until the first meeting of the Commission on or after September 1, 2010, and shall serve terms of four years thereafter. The Code Commissioners shall serve without compensation, but it shall be the duty of the County Mayor and the County Commission to provide for the payment by the county of all necessary and reasonable expenses, as determined by the County Commission,

Personal Notes and Position Papers

in its sole discretion, incurred by the Knox County Code Commission in carrying out the intent and purpose of this provision.

B. It shall be the duty of the Knox County Code Commission to provide for the codification and publication, in a bound volume, updated not less often than annually, of this Charter and all ordinances and emergency ordinances (hereafter collectively the "Knox County Code") of the Commission of Knox County. The Mayor shall cooperate with the Knox County Code Commission with respect to recommendations for contracts by Knox County with any law book publishers or other persons necessary and reasonable to implement this provision. The Commission shall annually appropriate funds to pay for the expenses of codification and costs of publication of the Knox County Code. Such code shall be made available for purchase by any person desiring same. Such Code, as published by the Knox County Code Commission, shall be prima facie evidence in all courts of the authenticity of such Charter, ordinances and emergency ordinances. All Courts of Knox County shall take judicial notice of this Charter and of county ordinances and emergency ordinances.

(Ref. of 11-7-06)

## ARTICLE IV. - OTHER OFFICERS [2]

[2] **Editor's note**— The referendum of November 7, 2006, added the provisions herein as article IV and subsequently renumbered the former articles IV—IX as articles V—X. The historical notation of the renumbered articles has been preserved for reference purposes. At the discretion of the editor, changes to internal references due to said renumbering have been included in brackets without notation.
Sec. 4.01. - Property Assessor.
Sec. 4.02. - Sheriff.
Sec. 4.03. - Register of Deeds.
Sec. 4.04. - County Clerk.
Sec. 4.05. - Trustee.
Sec. 4.06. - Elections and Filling Vacancies.

**Sec. 4.01. - Property Assessor.**

The duties of the Assessor of Property are vested in and exercised by the Knox County Property Assessor. The duties, qualifications, oath of office, bond requirements and compensation of the Assessor of Property shall be governed by the Constitution and laws of the State of Tennessee and the Knox County Charter. The duties of this office shall include, but not be limited to, the responsibility of determining and recording the value of all property within the county, whether real, personal or mixed, except for the property of public utilities valued by the State; provided, however, that nothing in this section shall diminish the duties of the Office of the Property Assessor as prescribed by the General Assembly, although additional duties may be given to this office by this Charter or by Ordinance of the County Commission.

(Ref. of 11-7-06)

Sec. 4.02. - Sheriff.

The duties of the Sheriff are vested in and exercised by the Knox County Sheriff, who shall be the Chief Law Enforcement Officer of Knox County. The duties, qualifications, oath of office, bond requirements, and compensation of the Knox County Sheriff shall be governed by the Constitution and laws of the State of Tennessee and the Knox County Charter. The general duties of Sheriff shall include, but not be limited to, being the Chief Law Enforcement Officer of Knox County, maintaining the jails of the County, providing courthouse and courtroom security and providing civil and criminal warrants service as well as those duties traditionally performed by the Sheriff in accordance with common law; provided, however, that nothing in this section shall diminish the duties of the Office of the Sheriff as prescribed by the General Assembly, although additional duties may be given to this office by this Charter or by Ordinance of the County Commission.

(Ref. of 11-7-06)

Sec. 4.03. - Register of Deeds.

The duties of the Register of Deeds are vested in and exercised by the Knox County Register of Deeds. The duties, qualifications, oath of office, bond requirements and compensation of the Register of Deeds shall be governed by the constitution and laws of the State of Tennessee and the Knox County Charter. The duties of this office shall include, but not be limited to, the responsibility for the filing or recordation of documents that affect the legal status of real or personal property; provided, however, that nothing in this section shall diminish the duties of the Office of the Register of Deeds as prescribed by the General Assembly, although additional duties may be given to this office by this Charter or by Ordinance of the County Commission.

(Ref. of 11-7-06)

### Sec. 4.04. - County Clerk.

The duties of the County Clerk are vested in and exercised by the Knox County Clerk. The duties, qualifications, oath of office, bond requirements, and compensation of the County Clerk shall be governed by the Constitution and laws of the State of Tennessee and the Knox County Charter. The general duties of this office shall include, but not be limited to, the responsibility for the collection of business taxes, motor vehicle registration and licensing, the collection of wheel taxes, the issuance of marriage and other licenses, and the keeping of records of the county's notaries public; provided, however, that nothing in this section shall diminish the duties of the Office of the County Clerk as prescribed by the General Assembly, although additional duties may be given to this office by this Charter or by Ordinance of the County Commission.

(Ref. of 11-7-06)

### Sec. 4.05. - Trustee.

The duties of the Trustee are vested in and exercised by the Knox County Trustee. The duties, qualifications, oath of office, bond requirements, and compensation of the Trustee shall be governed by the Constitution and laws of the State of Tennessee and the Knox County Charter. The general duties of this office shall include, but not be limited to, the responsibility for the collection of property taxes, the collection and disbursement of County funds, and the management of the county's cash flow and the investment of idle County funds; provided, however, that nothing in this section shall diminish the duties of the Office of the County Trustee as prescribed by the General Assembly, although additional duties may be given to this office by this Charter or by Ordinance of the County Commission.

(Ref. of 11-7-06)

### Sec. 4.06. - Elections and Filling Vacancies.

The officers listed in Article IV shall be elected by the voters of Knox County in accordance with the Constitution and general laws of the State of Tennessee and the Knox County Charter. Any vacancy in the offices listed in Article IV due to death, resignation, removal, or disability, the vacancy shall be filled by the Commission with a person meeting the qualifications for said position until his/her successor is elected in the next general election and sworn; provided, however, if such vacancy occurs within sixty (60) days prior to the next general election, the person so selected by the Commission to fill the vacancy shall serve the remainder of the term of that officer. Said selection shall not occur until such time as the Commission conducts a duly noticed public hearing during which time interested, qualified candidates will be interviewed by the Commission.

(Ref. of 11-7-06; Ref. of 8-5-10)

## ARTICLE V. - JUDICIAL BRANCH [3]

[3] Note— See editor's note at article IV.
Sec. 5.01. - Judiciary.
Sec. 5.02. - Vacancy.
Sec. 5.03. - Abolishing divisions or altering compensation.
Sec. 5.04. - Rules of court and evidence.
Sec. 5.05. - Reserved.
Sec. 5.06. - Fourth Circuit Court.
Sec. 5.07. - Juvenile Court.

### Sec. 5.01. - Judiciary.

A. The judiciary of Knox County Government shall be vested in the existing courts of Knox County or in any other courts established by law. Judges of the various courts of Knox County shall expressly continue as elective officers with all powers and duties conferred or implied by law upon their respective offices.

B. The Commission may, by ordinance, create such additional divisions of the General Sessions Court, as well as courts having such jurisdiction as is, or may hereafter be, provided by law, which it deems necessary and may abolish such divisions so long as the Commission shall comply with Section 4.03[5.03] of this Charter. Such additional divisions of the General Sessions Court may be given exclusive jurisdiction over County ordinance violations, and such other jurisdiction as may be authorized by all applicable laws of the State of Tennessee and this Charter.

### Sec. 5.02. - Vacancy.

If a vacancy occurs in any judicial office of the General Sessions or Juvenile Court, or in any other County judicial office established by law or by this Charter in Knox County, then that vacancy shall be filled by a vote of the Commission as prescribed in this Charter, and the person so selected shall serve until his/her successor is elected and sworn.

Personal Notes and Position Papers

**Sec. 5.03. - Abolishing divisions or altering compensation.**

Nothing herein shall grant to the Commission the power to abolish a division of any General Sessions Court, or any other County judicial office, during the term of office of a judge of that court, nor shall the Commission alter the compensation of any judge of any court of the County during the term of office of such judge. The Commission shall not abolish any division or alter the compensation of any judge for a subsequent term of any court of the County during the year in which an election of the judge of such court shall be held.

**Sec. 5.04. - Rules of court and evidence.**

Nothing herein contained shall confer upon the Commission the power to make rules of court, rules of evidence, or otherwise affect the rules of civil or criminal procedure applicable to the courts of Knox County. The power to make rules of court or rules of evidence shall be expressly reserved to the respective courts of Knox County, and/or to the Supreme Court of the State of Tennessee, and the Tennessee General Assembly, as applicable by law.

**Sec. 5.05. - Reserved.**

> **Editor's note—** Referendum of August 6, 2004, repealed § 4.05[5.05] in its entirety, which pertained to the Knox County Code Commission and derived from original codification.

**Sec. 5.06. - Fourth Circuit Court.**

There is hereby established the Circuit Court, Division IV of the Third Judicial Court of the State of Tennessee, hereinafter referred to as the Fourth Circuit Court for Knox County, Tennessee. The Fourth Circuit Court for Knox County, Tennessee, has previously been established by Chapter 265 of the Public Acts of 1965 and it is the intent of this Charter to continue said Court pursuant to the Act with full Charter status.

**Sec. 5.07. - Juvenile Court.**

There is hereby established the Juvenile Court of Knox County, Tennessee. The Juvenile Court of Knox County, Tennessee, has previously been established by Chapter 277 of the Private Acts of 1913, as amended, and it is the intent of this Charter to continue the Juvenile Court of Knox County, Tennessee, pursuant to the Act with full Charter status.

## ARTICLE VI. - EDUCATION [4]

[4] **Note—** See editor's note at article IV.
Sec. 6.01. - Board of Education.
Sec. 6.02. - Board duties and powers.
Sec. 6.03. - Board salary and compensation.
Sec. 6.04. - Superintendent of Schools.
Sec. 6.05. - Board of Education employees.

### Sec. 6.01. - Board of Education.

A. There is hereby created the Knox County Board of Education. The exclusive management and control of the school system of Knox County (hereinafter referred to as the "School System") is vested in the Knox County Board of Education (hereinafter referred to as either the "Board of Education" or the "Board"). The Board of Education members shall be elected by the people and shall take office on September 1 following their respective elections.

B. The Board of Education under this Charter shall consist of nine (9) members elected from nine (9) districts. The regular terms of the Board members shall be four (4) years with four (4) members elected at the time of the election of the County Assessor of Property and five (5) members elected at the time of the election of the Executive. In the event that the time of election of the County Assessor of Property shall be changed, by general law, to run concurrently with the other constitutional officers having four (4) year terms, the Commission, by ordinance, shall adopt a procedure to provide that all members of the Board of Education shall be elected at the same time and have concurrent terms.

C. At the County general election of 1990 a member of the Board of Education shall be elected for each of the school districts 1, 4, 6, 7 and 9 for terms of four (4) years. The members of the Board of Education from school districts 2, 3, 5 and 8 elected for four (4) year terms in the general election of 1988, as provided in Chapter 339 of the Private Acts of 1970, as amended, shall serve as members of the Board of Education until the County general election of 1992 at which time members of the Board of Education from such districts shall be elected for regular terms.

D. The districts of the members of the Board of Education shall be the districts as shall exist on December 31, 1989. The Board of Education, by resolution, may from time to time alter the boundaries of districts so long as all districts comply with constitutional

## Personal Notes and Position Papers

requirements. On or before December 31, 1991, and every ten (10) years thereafter, it shall be the duty of the Board of Education, based upon the most recent Federal decennial census, to reapportion the Board of Education districts so as to comply with constitutional requirements.

E. No person shall be eligible to serve as a member of the Board of Education unless that person shall have attained the age of eighteen (18) and is a resident of, and a registered voter in, the district from which such person seeks election on the date he/she filed his/her nominating petition and has been a resident of both the County and the district for one (1) year prior to such person's election; provided, however, that the district residency requirement shall not apply in the first general election at which a seat on the Board of Education appears on the ballot following a reapportionment of the Board districts. A member of the Board shall remain a resident of the Board district which such member represents during his/her term of office. No member of the Commission or any other public official or employee of the Board of Education shall be eligible for appointment or election to the Board of Education.

(Ref. of 8-1-96)

**Sec. 6.02. - Board duties and powers.**

A. The Board shall hold regular meetings at least monthly. The Chairman(woman) may call such special meetings when, in his/her judgment, the interest of the public schools require it or when requested to do so in writing by five (5) members of the Board.

B. The Board, at its first meeting on or after September 1, 1990, and annually thereafter, shall elect from its membership a Chairman(woman), Vice Chairman(woman), and such other officers as the Board deems necessary.

C. The Board shall have all such duties, powers and authority necessary or reasonably implied to manage and control the County School System as provided by Constitution, general law, this Charter or ordinance.

D. The Board may adopt such rules of order to govern its proceedings as it considers advisable and authorize such committees as necessary to carry out its responsibilities. Six (6) members of the Board shall constitute a quorum.

E. The Superintendent of Schools shall be the Secretary of the Board and the Executive Officer of the Board. The Chairman(woman) shall be the presiding officer of the Board and appoint all committees of the Board.

F. The Superintendent of Schools and the Chairman(woman) of the Board shall constitute the Executive Committee of the Board and shall meet as often as necessary to perform their duties. All actions of the Executive Committee shall be submitted to the Board at its meetings and shall be subject to ratification, modification or rejection by the Board.

G. All members of the Board shall give bond in an amount and under such terms as provided by law or ordinance.

**Sec. 6.03. - Board salary and compensation.**

Each member of the Board shall receive compensation in the same amount per month as provided for members of the Commission.

**Sec. 6.04. - Superintendent of Schools.**

A. The Superintendent of Schools (hereinafter sometimes referred to as the "Superintendent") shall be the chief administrative officer and executive official of the School System.

B. The Superintendent shall be responsible for the exercising of all executive and administrative functions of the School System. The Superintendent shall have all duties and exercise all powers and authority necessary to perform his/her responsibilities as authorized by general law, this Charter, ordinance, emergency ordinance or resolution.

C. The Superintendent of Schools shall be selected in accordance with State law.

D. No person shall be eligible to serve as Superintendent of Schools unless that person shall have attained the age of twenty-five (25) and has obtained the necessary education and certifications required by general law to hold such office. The Superintendent shall remain a resident of the County during his/her term of office.

E. The Superintendent of Schools shall receive annual compensation, paid in equal monthly installments, of not less than the amount provided by general law or not less than any elected County official, except the Mayor, whichever is greater.

(Ref. of 8-1-96; Ref. of 8-6-04)

### Sec. 6.05. - Board of Education employees.

Knox County adopts the Tennessee teacher tenure statutes. All employees of the Knox County School System not covered by the Tennessee teacher tenure statutes or separate contract shall be considered employees at will.

(Ref. of 8-6-04)

# ARTICLE VII. - PENSIONS [5]

(5) Note— See editor's note at article IV.
Sec. 7.01. - Continuation of present system.
Sec. 7.02. - Pension system.
Sec. 7.03. - Knox County Retirement and Pension Board.
Sec. 7.04. - Powers and duties.
Sec. 7.05. - Uniformed Officers Pension Plan.

### Sec. 7.01. - Continuation of present system.

Pursuant to the provisions of Chapter 246, Private Acts 1967-68, as amended, the County has established a local retirement system for County employees except for certified employees of the School System. The intent of this Charter is to continue such system with its powers and authority under this Charter.

### Sec. 7.02. - Pension system.

A. There is hereby created a system of pension and/or retirement and/or benefits for elected officials and employees of Knox County Government.

B. The intent of this Charter is to empower the Knox County Retirement and Pension Board (hereinafter sometimes referred to as the "Retirement Board") to design, adopt, administer and place into effect a financially sound retirement system and other benefits provided by ordinance.

C. The Retirement Board shall not adopt a policy, plan, plan amendment or administrative action unless it is actuarially sound and is actuarially funded at the time of adoption.

### Sec. 7.03. - Knox County Retirement and Pension Board.

A. The Knox County Retirement and Pension Board shall have nine (9) members. The members shall be the Mayor, four (4) members of the Commission to be selected by a majority vote of the membership thereof and four (4) current employees of Knox County who are participating members of the system.

B. The Commission shall select four (4) of its members to serve on the Knox County Retirement and Pension Board at its first session on or after September 1, 1990, and every four (4) years thereafter for terms of four (4) years concurrent with their terms as members of the Commission.

C. The Mayor shall serve as member of Knox County Retirement and Pension Board concurrently with his term as Executive.

D. The active participants in the Knox County Retirement and Pension System shall select two (2) active participants as members of the Retirement Board each two (2) years for four (4) year terms under such procedure as may be established by the Retirement Board. The terms of members elected by the participants shall begin on March 1 following their election. The terms of two (2) members elected by the participants shall begin on March 1, 1991 for four (4) year terms and two (2) participant members shall be elected for terms of two (2) years beginning on March 1, 1991. The participant members of the former Knox County Retirement and Pension Commission, established by Chapter 246 of the Private Acts of 1967-68, shall serve as members of the Retirement Board from the effective date of this Charter until participant members are elected as herein provided.

E. The members of the Retirement Board shall serve without compensation but may be reimbursed for any necessary and reasonable expenses incurred by them in the performance of their duties. A member of the Retirement Board shall not be prohibited from participating in the benefit or pension plans of any other retirement fund. Any vacancy in the membership of the Retirement Board shall be filled in the same manner as the original member to serve for the remainder of such term.

Personal Notes and Position Papers

F. A majority of the authorized membership of the Retirement Board shall constitute a quorum and all actions taken must be by a majority of the authorized membership. The Retirement Board shall, at its regular meeting in September, elect a Chairman(woman) and such other officers from its members as it deems appropriate for terms of one (1) year. The Retirement Board shall meet at least monthly in regular session, and special meetings may be called by the Chairman(woman) or by written request of a majority of the members.

(Ref. of 8-6-04)

Sec. 7.04. - Powers and duties.

A. The intent of this Charter is to continue the existing retirement and benefit plans established and administered under the provisions of Chapter 246 of the Private Acts of 1967-68 with minimal change as deemed appropriate and to transfer to a Charter-based authority.

B. The Retirement Board is empowered and shall have all necessary power and authority to design, adopt and administer a financially sound retirement system.

C. The Retirement Board is empowered to employ the services of legal counsel, investment consultants, actuarial consultants, and the services of others which it may deem necessary to maintain a soundly designed, administered and financed system.

D. The Retirement Board shall have complete control over the administration of the system and the rights of the participants to benefits thereunder and shall make any and all determinations, rulings and interpretations of the system in open meetings. The Retirement Board shall maintain records in accordance with generally accepted accounting principles applicable to governmental entities, and, for audit purposes, shall be considered as accounts of the County.

E. The Retirement Board shall not have the power or authority to adopt or approve any plan or plan amendment, or take any other action, which thereby would increase the funding or financial obligations of the County either at the time of the action or in the future without notification to and express consent and funding from the Commission by resolution. The intent of this provision is to restrict the power of the Retirement Board so that all plans, benefits, annuities or pensions are actuarially sound and actuarially funded from the date of their creation.

F. The Retirement Board shall annually file a financial report with the County Clerk showing all receipts, disbursements, liabilities and actuarial status of the system. The annual report and records of the Retirement Board shall be audited and reviewed by the County Auditor as any other fund of the County. All records of the Retirement Board shall be open for public inspection.

G. The provisions of the system designed by the former Retirement and Pension Commission under the provisions of Chapter 246 of the Private Acts of 1967-68 shall be the plan and system to be administered subject to amendment under the provisions thereof by the Retirement Board hereby created. The Retirement Board shall have full power to modify and amend such plan subject to the provision of Section 6.04.E[7.04.E] of this Charter.

H. All benefits payable to participants, retired participants, survivors, beneficiaries or otherwise, as lawfully adopted in the provisions of the system, shall continue unimpaired as provided therein and such benefits shall be an obligation of the Retirement Board and of Knox County.

I. Any person who shall knowingly make any false statements or shall falsify or permit to be falsified any record or records of the system in any attempt to defraud the system shall be guilty of a misdemeanor and upon conviction shall be punished accordingly and shall further forfeit any benefits under the provisions of the system. Any County elected official or employee who is convicted of a felony in the discharge of his/her county governmental duties shall forfeit any benefits under the provisions of the system.

### Sec. 7.05. - Uniformed Officers Pension Plan.

A. The Retirement Board is hereby authorized and directed to establish, maintain and administer as a plan of the system a separate, tax qualified, defined benefit pension plan and trust, known and designated as the Uniformed Officers Pension Plan (hereinafter referred to as the "Officers Pension") for sworn officers regularly employed by the Sheriff's Department.

B. The Officers Pension shall provide: (i) a normal retirement annuity for life, upon attainment of age 50 with at least 25 years of service, equal to 2.5% of average of high two 12-month periods salary times years of service, to a maximum of 30 years of service; (ii) after vesting upon completion of 5 years of service, early retirement after 25 years of service, disability and death benefits; provided that such disability and death benefits shall be

## Personal Notes and Position Papers

coordinated with and offset by other County-provided compensation, insurance or benefit arrangements; and provided further that the determination of disability under the Officers Pension shall be made on the basis of findings by an independent health care professional or organization selected by the Retirement Board; (iii) annual benefit adjustments of 3% per annum; and for retirees or beneficiaries over age 62, a further adjustment equal to one-half any annual change in the consumer price index over 3%, such further adjustment not to exceed 1% in any year; and (iv) a one-time, irrevocable choice for those initially eligible upon establishment of the Officers Pension: (a) to forego participation in the Officers Pension and to remain in any existing County plan in which they then currently participate; or (b) to waive all rights under such existing plans and to participate in the Officers Pension.

C. Participants shall contribute 6% of salary to the Officers Pension, which shall be picked up by the County. Accumulated balances of those initially eligible upon commencement of the Officers Pension who choose to participate in the Officers Pension shall be transferred, together with all associated liabilities for benefits, from any existing plan to the Officers Pension, but not including balances resulting from rollover contributions or excess voluntary employee contributions. The Retirement Board shall provide equitable, actuarially-sound procedures to be consistently applied to adjustments to Officer Pension benefits to account for any prior distribution from an existing plan to or on behalf of any Participant (including, by way of example but not as a limitation on the generality of the foregoing, a distribution upon a break in service or as a result of a qualified domestic relations order).

D. The actuary for the system shall annually compute and report normal and past service contributions for the Officers Pension, which report shall be considered by the Retirement Board and passed with the Board's recommendation to the Commission for acceptance and funding approval. The actuary shall also compute and report the unfunded actuarial accrued liability for the Officers Pension as of July 1, 2007, which report shall be considered by the Retirement Board and passed with the Board's recommendation to the Commission for acceptance and funding such that the Officers Pension shall be funded on an actuarially sound, and not necessarily actuarially funded, basis as of its date of commencement. The Officers Pension is not subject to, and is specifically hereby excepted from, the "actuarially funded" requirement contained in Sections 6.02(C)[7.02(C)] and 6.04(E)[7.04(E)] of the Knox County Charter.*

E. The Retirement Board shall adopt the Officers Pension to be effective July 1, 2007, subject to approval by the Commission by resolution, and the Retirement Board may thereafter amend the Officers Pension from time to time under the authority of Section 6.04(E)[7.04(E)], so long as any such amendment is consistent with the terms set out in this Section. The Officers Pension may not be terminated or rescinded except by amendment to the Charter.

*NOTE: The Knox County Retirement System projects the unfunded liability for the Pension to be approximately $57.1 million as of July 1, 2007, and, in addition, the County's expected additional annual cost of the Pension is projected to be about 5.9% of participant payroll, or $1.6 million the first year, over and above the 6% of participant payroll currently contributed by the County to the existing defined contribution retirement plan. The anticipated property tax impact is 8 cents per year.

(Ref. of 11-7-06)

# ARTICLE VIII. - ELECTIONS [6]

[6] **Note—** See editor's note at article IV.
Sec. 8.01. - Primary election required.
Sec. 8.02. - Date of primary.
Sec. 8.03. - Qualifying petitions.
Sec. 8.04. - Notice of election and other provisions.
Sec. 8.05. - Recall.

### Sec. 8.01. - Primary election required.

A primary election shall be held in Knox County for the selection of all political party nominees of all parties, which are qualified under State law as political parties, for the selection of candidates for all County offices, judicial offices and all other offices which are filled by the voters of Knox County at the August general election in even-numbered years. All such elections shall be held in the manner provided for holding such primary elections by general law.

### Sec. 8.02. - Date of primary.

The primary election to nominate candidates for the County general election shall be held on the first Tuesday in May next preceding the County August general election.

In years in which a Presidential Preference Primary is to be held in the State of Tennessee, the County Primary Election shall be held on the date selected by the Legislature for said Presidential Preference Primary. Where so authorized by State law, the County Commission may by Ordinance passed at least one (1) year before the proposed date, set the date for the County Primary on such date as the County Commission determines shall be the most economical and convenient for the citizens of Knox County.

(Ref. of 8-1-96)

### Sec. 8.03. - Qualifying petitions.

Any person deciding to submit his/her name to the voters in such primary election shall file a qualifying petition, in compliance with general law. The Election Commission shall verify the compliance of the petition with all requirements and declare the person a candidate and place his/her name on the primary ballot pursuant to general law.

In years in which a Presidential Preference Primary is to be held in the State of Tennessee, the qualifying position shall be filed no later than the date and time set forth for the filing of qualifying petitions for the Presidential Preference Primary. Where so authorized by law, the County Commission by Ordinance passed at least one (1) year before the date proposed, may set the date and time for filing qualifying petitions for the County Primary Election, provided that such date shall not be more than ninety (90) days preceding nor less than forty-five (45) days preceding the County Primary Election.

(Ref. of 8-1-96; Ref. of 11-7-06)

### Sec. 8.04. - Notice of election and other provisions.

All voters shall have the right to cast write-in ballots as provided by general law. The Election Commission shall give public notice of the election and employ officials to hold the primary as provided by general law. No person shall be placed on the ballot for any office in the August general election, subject to the provisions of this Article, and designated as a nominee of a political party, unless such person has received such nomination by virtue of having been selected as that party's candidate for such office in such County primary election except for replacement of candidates as provided by general law or when a vacancy occurs for which parties select nominees at a time in which compliance with the provisions of this Article is not possible.

### Sec. 8.05. - Recall.

(A)  This recall provision is applicable only to officials holding the positions of Knox County Mayor, County Commissioner, Law Director, Sheriff, County Clerk, Trustee, Register of Deeds, Property Assessor, and member of the Knox County Board of Education. The Judicial Branch, including the court clerks, are not subject to recall.

(B)  Such recall petition, process and recall election shall meet the requirements of state law.

(C)  Notwithstanding subsection (B), in the case of a recall of an official elected county-wide, the petition shall be signed by at least ten percent (10%) of those registered to vote in Knox County. However, in the case of a recall of a district county commissioner or member of the Board of Education, the petition shall be signed by at least ten percent (10%) of those registered to vote in the district represented by said official. The number of registered Knox County voters shall equal the number of voters registered in Knox County on January 1st of the calendar year the recall petition is filed with the Knox County Election Commission. No such petition shall be circulated until after the official has served one full year in office.

(D)  Notwithstanding subsection (B), the signed recall petition shall be filed with the Knox County Election Commission within ninety (90) days after final certification of the proper form of the petition by the Election Commission.

(E)  In a recall election, the following question shall be presented to each qualified voter:

> "Shall _____ (name of official) be recalled and removed from the Office of _____ (name of office).

(F)  If a majority of the voters vote "Yes," the incumbent shall be deemed recalled and removed from office upon the certification of the recall by the Knox County Election Commission.

(G)  In the event the incumbent is recalled, subject to Section (H) and pending the election provided for in Section (H), the County Commission shall fill the vacancy with a person meeting the qualifications for said office until his/her successor is elected, qualified, and sworn following the next general election.

## Personal Notes and Position Papers

(H) In the event the incumbent is recalled, an election to fill the vacancy shall be held at the next general election occurring at least sixty (60) days following certification of the recall. All such elections shall be held in the manner provided by law for holding a county general election as follows:

    (1) Political parties recognized under Tennessee Code, Title 2, Chapter 13 may nominate their candidates for office by any method authorized under the rules of the party.

    (2) Candidates not affiliated with a recognized political party shall be listed as independent.

    (3) The person elected to fill the vacancy created by the recall shall serve the remainder of the term of that office.

(I) It shall be a violation of the Knox County Charter, punishable by a fine of One Thousand Dollars ($1,000.00), for any person, directly or indirectly, personally or through any other person:

    (1) By force or threats to prevent or endeavor to prevent any qualified voter from signing or promoting a petition for recall;

    (2) To make use of any violence, force or restrain or to inflict or threaten the infliction of any injury, damage, harm or loss; or

    (3) In any manner to practice intimidation upon or against any person in order to induce or compel such person to sign or refrain from signing a petition for recall;

    (4) Any Knox County voter who has reasonable suspicion of the foregoing shall report said acts to the Knox County Election Commission and one of the following: the Knox County Sheriff, the District Attorney General, and the Knox County Law Director.

    (5) The General Sessions Court shall have jurisdiction of such Charter violation.

    (6) This Charter subsection is in addition to and does not supplant any provision of state law which may render any of these acts a felony or misdemeanor.

(J) If any section or provision of this recall provision shall be held unconstitutional, invalid or inapplicable to any persons or circumstances, then it is intended and declared by the people of the County that all other sections or provisions of this recall provision and their application to all other persons and circumstances shall be severable and shall not be affected by any such decision.

(K) This provision shall become effective on August 5, 2010.

(Ref. of 8-5-10)

> **Editor's note**— The referendum of August 5, 2010, replaced section 8.05 in its entirety to read as herein set out. Formerly, section 8.05 pertained to similar subject matter and derived from the referendum of August 7, 2008.

## ARTICLE IX. - GENERAL PROVISIONS [7]

[7] **Note**— See editor's note at article IV.
Sec. 9.01. - Title and filing of Charter.
Sec. 9.02. - Liberal construction of Charter.
Sec. 9.03. - Definitions.
Sec. 9.04. - Construction of words in this Charter.
Sec. 9.05. - Amendments to this Charter.
Sec. 9.06. - Discrimination prohibited.
Sec. 9.07. - Qualification and oath of elected officers.
Sec. 9.08. - Conflict of interest.
Sec. 9.09. - Bonding of officers and employees.
Sec. 9.10. - Residence and qualifications of County officials and employees.
Sec. 9.11. - Ex-officio members [of] boards, authorities, commissions, agencies.
Sec. 9.12. - Private Acts.
Sec. 9.13. - County seal and flag.
Sec. 9.14. - Service of process on County.
Sec. 9.15. - Health service.
Sec. 9.16. - Severability.
Sec. 9.17. - Term limits.

### Sec. 9.01. - Title and filing of Charter.

This Charter shall be known and may be cited as the "Charter of Knox County, Tennessee." Pursuant to T.C.A. § 5-1-209, the certified copy of the Charter of Knox County, Tennessee and the Proclamation of the Secretary of State of the State of Tennessee showing the result of the November 8, 1988 election shall be deposited with the County Clerk for permanent filing.

### Sec. 9.02. - Liberal construction of Charter.

The failure to mention a particular power or to enumerate similar powers of this Charter shall not be construed to exclude such a particular power or to restrict the authority that the County, as a public corporation, would have if the particular power is not mentioned or similar powers are not enumerated. This Charter shall be liberally construed to the end that, within the limits imposed by this Charter and by the Constitution and all applicable laws of the State of Tennessee, the County shall have all powers necessary and convenient for the conduct of its affairs, including all powers that counties may assume under the Constitution and all applicable laws of the State of Tennessee concerning home rule.

**Sec. 9.03. - Definitions.**

The following definitions shall be applicable:

 A. The phrase "administrative or executive act or function" shall mean any act or function either for or on behalf of the Knox County Government which is traditionally performed by the Chief Executive of a representative or republican form of government; provided, however, nothing in this definition shall be construed as prohibiting any officer, member or employee of the Commission in carrying out any act or functions necessary or desirable for the Commission to perform its legislative acts or functions.

 B. The words "emergency ordinance" shall mean any local legislation with regard to any subject within the definition of "ordinance" as provided in Section 8.03.D[9.03.D], of this Charter, adopted by the Commission in accordance with the formalities as set forth in this Charter and in all applicable laws of the State of Tennessee.

 C. The phrases "majority vote of the Commission" or "majority of the members (or membership) of the Commission" shall mean at least a majority of the membership of the Commission as provided in Section 2.03.B of this Charter.

 D. The word "ordinance," when used in connection with any action taken by the Commission, shall mean any local legislation adopted by that body which is adopted according to the formalities as set forth in this Charter and in all applicable laws of the State of Tennessee and is of a permanent nature in its effect, whether in a governmental or proprietary nature, and shall include, but not be limited to, any action which would have required Private Acts of the Tennessee General Assembly with constitutional ratification in the absence of this Charter.

E. The word "person" shall include both male and female, plural and singular, and shall include the terms "individual," "corporation," "partnership" and "association," unless reason dictates another construction.

F. A "reading" shall consist of a distinct and audible reading of the caption of an ordinance, emergency ordinance or resolution by either the Chairman(woman) of the Commission or the County Clerk and a copy of such ordinance, emergency ordinance or resolution being available for public inspection at such meeting and such other requirements as are provided by applicable law.

G. The word "resolution" shall mean any measure adopted by the Commission which is not either an ordinance or emergency ordinance, requiring a majority vote for passage, relating to subject matter of either a special or temporary nature, and shall specifically include, but not be limited to, the issuance of bonds, notes, other evidence of indebtedness and all matters relating thereto of the County.

H. The word "shall" shall be construed as mandatory, and the word "may" shall be construed as permissive.

I. The phrase "two-thirds (2/3) of the members (or membership) of the Commission" shall mean at least two-thirds (2/3) of the membership of the Commission as provided in Section 2.03.B of this Charter.

**Sec. 9.04. - Construction of words in this Charter.**

As used in this Charter, all masculine pronouns shall also mean the feminine; where reason dictates, the singular shall also include the plural.

**Sec. 9.05. - Amendments to this Charter.**

A. In the manner provided by law for the framing, proposal and submission of new charters, a Charter Commission may frame and propose amendment(s) to this Charter and shall submit any such amendment(s) to the voters of the County.

B. The Commission of Knox County may frame and, by a favorable vote of two-thirds (2/3) of the Commission, propose amendments to this Charter. Except as otherwise provided in this Subsection, every ordinance proposing a Charter amendment shall be introduced in the form and manner, and governed by the

## Personal Notes and Position Papers

procedure and requirements, prescribed for ordinances generally. Every such ordinance proposing a Charter amendment shall contain, after the enacting clause, the following, and no other matter: (1) a statement that the Charter amendment set out in the ordinance is proposed for submission to the voters of the County in accordance with the requirements of this Charter, and (2) the full text of the proposed Charter amendment. Such an ordinance shall become effective upon adoption, and its effect shall be to require that the County Clerk immediately deliver a certified copy of the ordinance to the County Election Commission and that the Election Commission submit the proposed Charter amendment, therein contained, to the voters of the County as provided in Section 8.05.E[9.05.E].

C. Voters of the County may frame and propose amendments to this Charter by a petition addressed to the Commission, which petition shall contain the information required by Section 9.05.B for ordinances proposing amendments, and no other matter except as hereinafter provided in this Section 9.05.C. Notwithstanding the provisions of Section 2-5-151(d) of the Tennessee Code Annotated, any petition proposing a Charter amendment must be filed with the County Clerk and must be signed by qualified voters of the County equal in number to at least fifteen percent (15%) of the persons who voted in the last gubernatorial election in Knox County. The County Clerk shall immediately deliver said petition to the County Election Commission. When the County Election Commission determines that such petitions are legally sufficient, it shall submit same to the voters of the County in accordance with Section 9.05.E.

D. On or before March 1, 1996, and on or before January 1 of each eight (8) years thereafter, there shall be constituted a Charter Review Committee for the purpose of reviewing this Charter and determining the desirability of amendment(s) thereto. The Charter Review Committee shall be composed of twenty-seven (27) total members with one (1) member of the Commission from each Commission district to be nominated by the Knox County Commission, nine (9) citizen members who are registered voters of Knox County and who are not members of the Commission to be nominated by the Knox County Commission and nine (9) citizen members who are registered voters of Knox County who are not members of the Commission to be nominated by the Knox County Mayor. Not more than two (2) such citizen members who are registered voters of Knox County shall be nominated from each Commission district. Each nominee shall be voted upon individually by the Knox County Commission. In the event a nominee does not receive a majority of votes, then the person who nominated said nominee shall bring forth a different nominee. It shall be the duty of the Charter Review Committee to give ample opportunity to County officeholders and members of the general public to make suggested changes to this Charter. In accordance with state law, the Charter Review commission shall either: (1) certify to the Knox County Election Commission such amendment(s) which it has determined to be desirable; or (2) certify to the Mayor and to the County Commission a statement that it does not recommend amending this Charter.

E. Any and all proposed charter amendments to be submitted to the voters of the County shall be submitted to the Knox County Election Commission in accordance with state law. The County Election Commission shall submit any Charter amendments certified and delivered to it, in accordance with the provisions of this Section 9.05, to the voters of the county at the next regular State or County election following the delivery to the County Election Commission of the ordinance or petition proposing the amendment. Not less than three (3) weeks before any election at which a proposed Charter amendment is to be voted on, the Election Commission shall publish a notice of the proposed amendment(s), in the form as provided by law, in a daily newspaper of general circulation in the County. The form of the ballot for submission of proposed Charter amendments shall be governed by the laws of the State of Tennessee concerning referendum elections. If a majority of the voters of the County voting upon a proposed Charter amendment votes in favor of it, the amendment shall become effective at the time fixed in the amendment or, if no time is therein fixed, thirty (30) days after its adoption by the voters of the County. Any Charter amendment shall be published promptly after its adoption in the manner provided in this Charter for adopted ordinances.

(Ref. of 8-6-04; Ref. of 8-7-08; Ref. of 11-4-08)

**Sec. 9.06. - Discrimination prohibited.**

A. No elected official, administrator, director, or employee of Knox County shall discriminate against any person in employment or provision of services based upon race, sex, religion, age or nationality without due process of law. The Commission, by ordinance, or in the absence of ordinance, the Mayor, by executive order, may establish such processes and procedures as may be deemed necessary to carry out the provisions of this Section. The Commission shall, by ordinance or resolution, take any action which it deems appropriate to ameliorate any condition or circumstance created by, or resulting from, any one or more violations of the provisions of this Section.

B.  The Mayor shall designate an administrative official to:

   (1)  enforce ordinances or resolutions adopted by the Commission pursuant to this Section;

   (2)  review practices of the Knox County Government to insure compliance with this Section 8.06[9.06] and all applicable Federal and State laws; and

   (3)  investigate complaints and claims of violations of this Section or of applicable State or Federal laws relating to equal employment practices.

(Ref. of 8-6-04)

### Sec. 9.07. - Qualification and oath of elected officers.

Before entering upon their duties, every officer whose election or appointment is prescribed in this Charter shall meet all qualifications provided by this Charter and all applicable laws of the State of Tennessee and shall take and subscribe to the following oath or affirmation before a person authorized to administer oaths:

> I do solemnly swear (or affirm) that I will support, obey and defend the Constitution of the United States, the Constitution of the State of Tennessee, and the Charter of Knox County, Tennessee, and that I will faithfully discharge the duties of my office to the best of my ability.

Any person refusing to take the oath or affirmation shall forfeit that office immediately.

### Sec. 9.08. - Conflict of interest.

A.  It shall be unlawful for any member of the Commission, the Mayor, other elected officeholder, or any administrative assistant, executive assistant, head of any division or department of County Government, or any other person employed by the County to vote for, let out, overlook, or in any manner to superintend any work or contract with the County for the sale of any land, materials, supplies, or services to, or by, the County, or to a contractor supplying the County, where such person has a substantial financial interest, direct or indirect, as defined by T.C.A. § 12-4-101, and any subsequent amendment thereto.

B.  Any person who willfully conceals such a substantial financial interest or willfully violates the requirements of this Section shall be guilty of malfeasance in office or position and shall be subject to ouster from office or termination of employment. Violation of this Section with the knowledge, express or implied, of the person or corporation contracting with or making a sale to the County shall render the contract voidable by the Mayor or the Commission.

C. Any member of the Commission who is also an employee of the County may vote on matters in which he has a conflict of interest arising from his/her employment with the County if the member informs the Commission immediately prior to the vote as follows: "Because I am an employee of (name of governmental unit), I have a conflict of interest in the proposal about to be voted. However, I declare that my argument and my vote answer only to my conscience and to my obligation to my constituents and to the citizens this body represents."

**Note**—See editor's note at the end of this section.

D. In the event a member of the Commission has a conflict of interest in a matter to be voted upon by the body, he/she may abstain for cause by announcing such to the presiding officer.

E. The vote of any member of the Commission having a conflict of interest who does not inform the Commission of such conflict shall be void if challenged by a member of the Commission in a timely manner and ruled to be a conflict of interest by the Chairman(woman) of the Commission. As used in this Section, "timely manner" shall mean during the same meeting at which the vote was cast and prior to the transaction of any further business by the body.

F. No elected or appointed official or employee of Knox County shall advocate, recommend, supervise, manage or cause the employment, appointment, promotion, transfer, or advancement of his or her relative to an office or position of employment within the Knox County government.

For the purposes of this policy, "relative" means parent, step-parent, foster parent, parent-in-law, child, spouse, brother, brother-in-law, foster brother, step-brother, sister, sister-in-law, foster sister, step-sister, grandparent, son-in-law, daughter-in-law, grandchild or other person who resides in the same household. A court-appointed legal guardian or an individual who has acted as a parent substitute is also included within this definition.

G. (i) An elected official or employee of Knox County with responsibility to vote on a measure shall disclose during the meeting at which the vote takes place, before any discussion or vote on the measure and so it appears in the minutes, any personal interest that affects or that would lead a reasonable person to infer that it affects the official's vote on the measure. In addition, said elected official or employee shall recuse him/herself from the discussion and/or vote on the matter. This provision shall not be applicable to voting on measures for reappointment of districts or other measures that affect all members of the Knox County Commission.

> (ii) "Personal Interest" means, for the purposes of disclosure of personal interests in accordance with this policy, a financial interest of the official or employee, or a financial interest of the official's or employee's spouse or child living in the same household, in the matter to be voted upon, regulated, supervised, or otherwise acted upon in an official capacity.

(Ref. of 8-6-04; Ref. of 11-4-08)

Editor's note—See note at the end of Section 2.03.

**Sec. 9.09. - Bonding of officers and employees.**

The Mayor and such other County officers and employees, as the Commission may provide, shall give bond in the amount and in the surety form prescribed by the Commission. The premiums of such bonds shall be paid by the County.

(Ref. of 8-6-04)

**Sec. 9.10. - Residence and qualifications of County officials and employees.**

A.   Any County official who shall voluntarily remove his/her residence outside the district from which elected or appointed shall forfeit that office immediately.

B.   Any lawyer, either elected or employed by the County in a legal or judicial capacity, who is suspended or barred from the practice of law in the State of Tennessee, shall forfeit that office immediately and shall not hold office or be reemployed during the term of such suspension or disbarment.

### Sec. 9.11. - Ex-officio members [of] boards, authorities, commissions, agencies.

No County officer or employee who is compensated for his/her service by salary shall receive any additional salary for serving as an ex-officio member of a County board, commission, authority or agency.

### Sec. 9.12. - Private Acts.

All Private Acts of the General Assembly of Tennessee, either referenced and/or included in this Charter by paraphrase, shall be, and remain, a part of this Charter with full Charter status. Between September 1, 1990 and September 1, 1991, it shall be the duty of the Law Director and the Commission to review all Public Acts having local application to Knox County, and all Private Acts which affect Knox County, of the General Assembly of the State of Tennessee, not in conflict with the provisions of this Charter, for the purpose of the Commission enacting ordinances to replace such Acts as the Commission, in its sole discretion, shall determine to be in the public welfare; provided, however, the Commission shall enact such ordinances, either replacing such Acts or continuing such Acts in full force and effect, where any such Acts constitute the authority for Knox County to continue to levy taxes and/or where such Act constitutes, or forms the basis of, any continuing obligation of Knox County or of any department, agency, authority or commission thereof. All other Public Acts with local application to Knox County, and all Private Acts which affect Knox County, of the General Assembly of the State of Tennessee, shall become null and void and of no further force and effect from and after September 1, 1991.

### Sec. 9.13. - County seal and flag.

The Commission shall have the power either to adopt an official seal and flag for the County or to continue the same seal and flag from the previous County Government.

### Sec. 9.14. - Service of process on County.

Service of any legal process, notice, or other matter to be served upon the County pursuant to any rule, regulation or law shall be made upon the Mayor or as authorized by law.

(Ref. of 8-6-04)

## Personal Notes and Position Papers

**Sec. 9.15. - Health service.**

A. The County may acquire, construct, equip, extend, repair, maintain and manage, or contract for management, and operate, or cause to be operated through contract, hospitals, clinics, and nursing homes and other extended care facilities owned, supported or controlled by the County.

B. The County may act through a nonprofit corporation or authority established by it to accomplish or carry out any or all of the above-outlined duties.

**Sec. 9.16. - Severability.**

If any article, section or provision of this Charter shall be held unconstitutional, invalid or inapplicable to any persons or circumstances, then it is intended and declared by the people of the County that all other articles, sections or provisions of this Charter and their application to all other persons and circumstances shall be severable and shall not be affected by any such decision.

**Sec. 9.17. - Term limits.**

A. Effective January 1, 1995, no person shall be eligible to serve in any elected office of Knox County if during the previous two terms of that office the person in question has served more than a single term. Service prior to the passage of this measure shall not count in determining length of service. Judges are exempt from this provision.

B. In January prior to each state legislative session until such a time that it can be certified that the legislative term limits described in this clause have been enacted, the clerk shall write all state legislators whose districts include any part of Knox County stating that the people of Knox County desire an opportunity to vote on legislative term limits. The people of Knox County respectfully request that a proposed constitutional amendment limit each Representative to six years (three terms) in the Tennessee House of Representatives and eight years (two terms) in the Tennessee Senate. The people of Knox County also instruct all state legislators representing any part of Knox County to pass this proposed constitutional amendment and place it on the general election ballot.

C. In January of each year until such a time that it can be certified that the term limits described in this clause have been enacted, the clerk of Knox County shall write all U.S.

Representatives whose districts include any part of Knox County's limits and both federal Senators stating that the people of this municipality support term limits for the U.S. Congress. The people of Knox County respectfully request that a proposed federal constitutional amendment limit each Representative to six years (three terms) in the United States House of Representatives and twelve years (two terms) in the United States Senate. The people of this municipality also instruct their federal delegation to pass a constitutional amendment imposing these limits and submit it to the states for ratification.

D. If any provision of this petition shall be held unconstitutional, invalid or inapplicable to any persons or circumstances, then it is intended and declared by the people of the County that all other provisions of this petition and their application to all other persons and circumstances shall be severable and shall not be affected by such decision.

(Ref. of 11-8-94)

## ARTICLE X. - TRANSITION PROVISIONS [8]

[8] **Note—** See editor's note at article IV.
Sec. 10.01. - Repeal of contrary laws.
Sec. 10.02. - Prior resolutions, orders and regulations.
Sec. 10.03. - Pending matters.
Sec. 10.04. - Judicial and other proceedings.
Sec. 10.05. - Rights and obligations.
Sec. 10.06. - Elected and appointed officers.
Sec. 10.07. - Zoning.
Sec. 10.08. - Referendum.
Sec. 10.09. - Effective date.

**Sec. 10.01. - Repeal of contrary laws.**

This Charter shall occupy the entire field of self-government for Knox County allowed by the Constitution of the State of Tennessee, and all public acts, private acts, ordinances, resolutions, orders, regulations, proclamations and any other enactment of any nature whatsoever, legislative, executive or judicial, local in effect, which are in force when this Charter becomes effective, are hereby repealed to the extent that they are inconsistent with, or interfere with, the effective operation of this Charter or of the ordinances, emergency ordinances or resolutions adopted by the Commission pursuant to the provisions of this Charter.

Personal Notes and Position Papers

**Sec. 10.02. - Prior resolutions, orders and regulations.**

All resolutions, orders, regulations and directives of the former County government, of whatsoever branch, division or department, which are in full force and effect at the time this Charter takes effect, to the extent that they are not inconsistent with the provisions of this Charter, shall remain in full force and effect until altered, modified or repealed in accordance with this Charter.

**Sec. 10.03. - Pending matters.**

All matters pending before, or under consideration by, the former Board of County Commissioners at the time this Charter takes effect, to the extent they are not inconsistent with the provisions of this Charter, may be acted upon, and disposed of, as if they had originated and had been introduced under this Charter.

**Sec. 10.04. - Judicial and other proceedings.**

All judicial proceedings of any kind or character, either by or against the County, and all proceedings to incur debt, whether by notes, bonds or other evidences of indebtedness, begun or pending at the time this Charter takes effect, all contracts for the doing of any kind of public work, not completed and performed at the time this Charter takes effect, and all contracts or bids for the purchase or sale of property entered into prior to the time this Charter takes effect, but not consummated at such time, shall in no way be affected by the adoption of this Charter, but the same may be completed in every respect as nearly as may be in accordance with the provisions of this Charter.

**Sec. 10.05. - Rights and obligations.**

All rights of action, contracts, obligations, titles, fines, penalties, forfeitures, and fees, accrued to or in favor of, or against, the County, at the time this Charter takes effect, shall remain in existence in full force and effect as fully as though this Charter had not taken effect. All recognizances, contracts and obligations lawfully entered into or executed by, or to, the County, and the lien thereof, all taxes due or owing to the County, and the lien thereof, and all writs, prosecutions, actions and causes of action shall continue and remain unaffected by this Charter.

**Sec. 10.06. - Elected and appointed officers.**

All officers elected or appointed for definite terms, prior to the effective date of this Charter, shall continue to hold office without abridgement of term or reduction of salary, unless lawfully removed, until their respective successors are duly elected, or appointed, and sworn.

**Sec. 10.07. - Zoning.**

This Charter shall not alter or change zoning regulations effective in the County, but the same shall continue until modified, altered, amended or repealed by the Commission acting under authority granted in this Charter.

**Sec. 10.08. - Referendum.**

This Charter shall be submitted by the Knox County Election Commission to the vote of the qualified voters of Knox County, Tennessee, at an election to be held on November 8, 1988. The ballots used in such election shall contain the following, and no further or different words:

"SHALL KNOX COUNTY GOVERNMENT BE CHANGED FROM ITS CURRENT FORM TO A HOME RULE CHARTER GOVERNMENT CONSISTING OF AN EXECUTIVE BRANCH HEADED BY THE EXECUTIVE OF KNOX COUNTY, A LEGISLATIVE BRANCH CONSISTING OF THE COMMISSION OF KNOX COUNTY AND A JUDICIAL BRANCH CONSISTING OF THE EXISTING COURTS OF KNOX COUNTY, OR ANY OTHER COURTS ESTABLISHED BY LAW?

FOR A CHARTER FORM OF COUNTYGOVERNMENT .....

AGAINST A CHARTER FORM OF COUNTY

GOVERNMENT ....."

**Sec. 10.09. - Effective date.**

This Charter shall become effective September 1, 1990, and shall be effective prior thereto to the extent necessary to permit primaries and elections to be held as otherwise provided herein during the year 1990. Article VII of this Charter, relating to nominations and elections, shall apply to the nomination and election of all officers required to be elected under this Charter commencing with the primary and general elections for the year 1990.

# Work Cited

Abraham, N., Hall, J., & VanMetr, B. (2009). First-Class Inefficiency. *Forbes Magazine.*

Adams, J. (1798a). Letter to Officers of the First Brigade of the Third Division of the Militia of Massachusetts. *October, 11*(1798), 265-266.

Adams, J. (1798b). Letter to the Officers of the First Brigade of the Third Division of the Militia of Massachusetts. In.

Alesina, A., & Tabellini, G. (2007). Bureaucrats or politicians? Part I: a single policy task. *American Economic Review, 97*(1), 169-179.

Alexandar, A. (2011). Citizen legislators or political musical chairs: Term limits in California.

Amar, V. D. (2009). Lessons from California's Recent Experience with Its Non-Unitary (Divided) Executive of Mayors, Governors, Controllers, and Attorneys. *Emory Law Journal, 59*(2).

Augenblick, N., & Nicholson, S. (2016). Ballot position, choice fatigue, and voter behaviour. *The Review of Economic Studies, 83*(2), 460-480.

Bailey, B. (2011, April 7, 2011). *Knox County fee office resolution hits snag.* WBIR.

Bailey, B. (2012, April 27, 2012). *Indictments renew old questions about Knox County fee offices.* WBIR.

Beeler, R. (2012). Oh, those unintended consequences. *The Knoxville Focus.*

Berry, C. R., & Gersen, J. E. (2008). The unbundled executive. *U. Chi. L. Rev., 75*, 1385.

Birnbaum, J. H. (2001). Mr. CEO goes to Washington. *FORTUNE, 143*(6), 140-+.

Board, E. (1995). Marion Barry's Sour Legacy. *New York Times.*

Board, E. (2012a). Finance director must prove worth to taxpayers. *Knoxville News Sentinel.*

Board, E. (2012b). Knox County Mayor Tim Burchett learns hard lesson in perils of cronyism. *Knoxville News Sentinel.*

Board, E. (2012c). Time to revisit appointing some Knox offices. *Knoxville News Sentinel.*

Board, E. R. (2012, April 11, 2012). Editorial: Charter Review Committee turns to serious business. *Knoxville News Sentinel.*

Bonavita, J. (2012). *Agenda for May 9 Charter Review Committee Meeting.*

Briggs, R. (2012a). Control of budgets, funds and salaries of the Knox County Sheriff, Trustee, Register, County Clerk and Property Assessor. In.

Briggs, R. (2012b). Response to memorandum of Knox County Law Director dated March 18, 2009. In.

Buffer, M. (2011, November 6, 2011). Voters face ballot fatigue at the polls. *The Citizen's Voice.*

Bullock III, C. S., & Dunn, R. E. (1996). Election roll-off: A test of three explanations. *Urban Affairs Review, 32*(1), 71-86.

Burnett, C. M., & Kogan, V. (2010). The Case of the Stolen Initiative: Were the Voters Framed. Annual Meeting of the American Political Science Association (2–5 December), Washington, DC, USA,

Burnett, C. M., & Kogan, V. (2012). Familiar choices: reconsidering the institutional effects of the direct initiative. *State Politics & Policy Quarterly, 12*(2), 204-224.

Burnham, W. D. (1965). The changing shape of the American political universe. *American Political Science Review, 59*(1), 7-28.

Buuck, D. (2012). Law Director's Office. In.

Campbell, A., Converse, P. E., Miller, W. E., & Stokes, D. E. (1960). The American Voter. New York: lohn Wiley & Sons. *Inc. CampbellThe American Voter1960.*

Caudill, C. B., & Peak, K. J. (2009). Retiring from the thin blue line: A need for formal preretirement training. *FBI L. Enforcement Bull., 78*, 1.

Chartrand, S. (2004). Patents; The patent office argues that the government should just let it live off what it gets from inventors. *New York Times.*

Chen, D. B., M. (2008, September 10, 2008). Across County, New Challenges to Term Limits. *New York Times.*

Counties, N. A. o. *History of County Government*.
Counties, N. A. o. (1999). *Who's Elected and Who's Appointed* [Research Brief].
*County Leadership Handbook 2008: Special Edition, National Association of Counties, Revised March 2011*.
Court rejects J. M. Smucker's PB&J patent. (2005, April 8, 2005).
Craig, T. (2011). Okay to put friends in city jobs, Barry says. *Washington Post*.
Deno, K. T., & Mehay, S. L. (1987). Municipal management structure and fiscal performance: Do city managers make a difference? *Southern Economic Journal*, 627-642.
*Detailed Review of Retirement Plan Trends, Best Practices, and Innovations by Other Public and Private-Sector Employers*. (2008). Price Waterhouse Cooper
Donila, M. (2011a). Audit: Misused funds, oversight lapses rampant in Knox County solid waste office. *Knoxville News Sentinel*.
Donila, M. (2011b). Change to Knox County fee offices on the table. *Knoxville News Sentinel*.
Donila, M. (2011c). Knox residents assumed immediate $57 million obligation with enhanced pension vote. *Knoxville News Sentinel*.
Donila, M. (2011d, October 16, 2011). Studies don't agree on law enforcement's mortality rate. *Knoxville News Sentinel*.
Donila, M. (2012). Rep. Frank Niceley: Time to Get Rid of City-County Planning Commission. *Knoxville News Sentinel*.
Dubin, J. A., & Kalsow, G. A. (1996). Comparing absentee and precinct voters: Voting on direct legislation. *Political Behavior*, *18*, 393-411.
Dubin, J. A., & Kalsow, G. A. (1997). *Participation in direct legislation: Evidence from the voting booth*. California Institute of Technology.
Editorial. (2006). Patently Ridiculous. *New York Times*.
Ferrar, R. (2008, November 4, 2008). Charter amendment #3 appears to win, barely; #4 rejected. *Knoxville News Sentinel*.
Ferrar, R. (2011a). Change at Knox County Fee Offices Delayed. *Knoxville News Sentinel*.

Ferrar, R. (2011b). Compromise covers Knox County fee officers' budgets; Burchett: Deal 'accomplishes all our goals'. *Knoxville News Sentinel.*

Ferrar, R. (2011c). Cynthia Finch gets probation for forgery counts. *Knoxville News Sentinel.*

Follick, J. (2008). Budget blues lead lawmakers to eye-raising cigarette tax. *Ocala.com.*

Gordon, T. (2011). California's Initiative Turns 100: Initiatives Aren't as Bad as You Think.

Greenhouse, S. (2011). Postal service is nearing default as losses mount. *New York Times.*

Group, P. A. (2000). Should we elect or appoint county officials? In: The Texas Association of Counties.

Hayek, F. A. (1944). *The Road to Serfdom.* University of Chicago Press.

Henchman, J., & Greaves, T. (2009). *Charging Taxpayers for Tax Collection Is a Tax.* Tax Foundation.

Henderson, B. (2002). Bean v. Quist: A Simple Court Clerkship Can Stir Up Quite a Political Stew. *Metro Pulse.*

Holgate, S. (2004). US Voters Elect Officials from Dogcatcher to President: Diversity of Elective Posts a Hallmark of American Democracy. *Washington File.*

Hoover, G. A. (2008). Elected versus appointed school district officials: Is there a difference in student outcomes? *Public Finance Review, 36*(5), 635-647.

Jacoby, J. E. (1997). The American prosecutor in historical context. *The Prosecutor, 31*(3), 33.

Jarrett, J. (2011). Regarding the Fee Officer Resolution. *Memorandum to Knox County Commission.*

Jarrett, J. (2012). Discuss of Fee Office Salary Suit Process. In D. Page (Ed.).

Johnston, D. (1996). House Report on Travel Office Attacks Clinton. *New York Times.*

Kalt, B. C. (2011). Politics and the Federal Appointments Process. *Harvard Law & Policy Review Online.*

Keane, A. G. (2012). Postal Service Says It Will Exhaust Cash Without Help. *Bloomberg Businessweek.*

Key, V. O. (1966). *The responsible electorate: Rationality in presidential voting 1936–1960.* Harvard University Press.

Kimball, D. C., & Kropf, M. (2008). Voting technology, ballot measures, and residual votes. *American Politics Research, 36*(4), 479-509.

## Personal Notes and Position Papers

Kirsch, I. S. (1994). *Adult literacy in America*. DIANE Publishing.

League, N. C. (2011). *Guide for Charter Commissions*.

Lewis, E. E. (1980). Public entrepreneurship: Toward a theory of bureaucratic political power: the organizational lives of Hyman Rickover, J. Edgar Hoover, and Robert Moses. *(No Title)*.

Lineberry, R. L., & Fowler, E. P. (1967). Reformism and public policies in American cities. *American Political Science Review, 61*(3), 701-716.

MacDonald, L. (2008). The impact of government structure on local public expenditures. *Public Choice, 136*, 457-473.

Mackay, G. (2012). Re: Ballot Fatigue Whitepaper. In D. Page (Ed.).

Madison, D. (1999). How did Cathy Quist, clerk of Circuit and General Session Court, become a political bullseye? *Metro Pulse Online*.

Madison, J. (2016). The Federalist Papers. In *Democracy: A Reader* (pp. 52-57). Columbia University Press.

Marinucci, C. (2004). Same-sex weddings used as rallying point. *San Francisco Chronicle*.

McGlynn, A. J., & Sylvester, D. E. (2010). Assessing the effects of municipal term limits on fiscal policy in US cities. *State and Local Government Review, 42*(2), 118-132.

Meletta, L.-B. C. (2007). Non-Enforcement by a Local Executive: Limitations of Judicial Review and Considerations to Restrain the Use of Executive Power. *NYU Ann. Surv. Am. L., 63*, 511.

Mill, J. S. (1989). *JS Mill:'On Liberty'and Other Writings*. Cambridge University Press.

Mingus, M. S. (2007). The new public management and democracy in Canada: A recipe for scandal. *Leading the Future of the Public Sector: The Third Transatlantic Dialogue*.

Moon, M. (2009). *Taxes vs. Fees: What's the Difference Between Bananas and Driver's Licenses?* Tax Foundation.

Morgan, D. R., & Kickham, K. (1999). Changing the form of county government: Effects on revenue and expenditure policy. *Public Administration Review*, 315-324.

Morgan, D. R., & Pelissero, J. P. (1980). Urban policy: does political structure matter? *American Political Science Review, 74*(4), 999-1006.

Mueller, J. E. (1969). Voting on the propositions: Ballot patterns and historical trends in California. *American Political Science Review, 63*(4), 1197-1212.

Munnell, A. H., Haverstick, K., & Soto, M. (2007). Why have defined benefit plans survived in the public sector. In: State and Local Pension Plans.

Neale, T. H. (2009). Presidential Terms and Tenure: Perspectives and Proposals for Change.

Negroponte, N. (1995). *Being digital*. Vintage.

Nocera, J. (2012). Free the Post Office! *New York Times*.

Olsen, D. (2006, October 6, 2006). Amending city charter a lengthy issue. *Craig Daily Press*.

Onorato Presents 2009 Comprehensive Fiscal Plan. (2008). *Allegheny County News Release*.

Ostrom, V. (2008). *The intellectual crisis in American public administration*. University of Alabama Press.

Ostrom, V., & Ostrom, E. (1971). Public choice: A different approach to the study of public administration. *Public Administration Review, 31*(2), 203-216.

Rauch, J. E. (1994). Bureaucracy, infrastructure, and economic growth: Evidence from US cities during the progressive era. In: National Bureau of Economic Research Cambridge, Mass., USA.

Reilly, S., & Richey, S. (2011). Ballot question readability and roll-off: The impact of language complexity. *Political Research Quarterly, 64*(1), 59-67.

Reilly, S., Richey, S., & Taylor, J. B. (2012). Using Google search data for state politics research: an empirical validity test using roll-off data. *State Politics & Policy Quarterly, 12*(2), 146-159.

Rolando, F. (2011). Crippled by a Mandate. *New York Times*. (Room for Debate Series)

Sack, K. (1995). Pataki Hiriing Is Criticized as Cronyism. *New York Times*.

Sanford, P., Hudson, B., O'Looney, J., & Gordon, R. (2012). *Responding to the new realities: Case studies in county governance*.

Schmid, J. (2009). Congress deals funding blow to Patent Office Budget strips $100 million provision for backlogged agency. *Journal Sentinel*.

Schmid, J., & Poston, B. (2009). Patent backlog clogs recovery: Agency's inability to keep pace undermines American innovation, competitiveness. *Journal Sentinel*.

Segal, D. (2011). Cities Turn to Fees to Fill Budget Gaps"The New York Times. In.

Shaw, B. (2019). *Maxims for revolutionists*. Good Press.

*Shelby County Charter*. Shelby County, Tennessee

Skelton, G. (2007). Gov.'s about-face on healthcare `fees' is more than a matter of semantics. *LA Times*.

Staff. (2007). Fenty proposes raising 911 'fee'. *The Washington Times*.

Staff. (2012, July 25, 2012). Proposal to close Knox Sheriff's Office pension plan to be on Nov. ballot. *Knoxville News Sentinel*.

Stewar, N. (2011). Gray defends controversial hires and salaries. *Washington Post*.

Stolberg, S. G., & Rutenberg, J. (2006). Rumsfeld resigns as defense secretary after big election gains for democrats. *New York Times*, 8.

Sullivan, J. (2011). Knox County fees offices not following Charter budgetary provisions. *Metro Pulse*.

Sumerford, H. (2010). Lockett pleads guilty to embezzlement, resigns as Knox law director. In: WATE.

Tarr, G. A. (2018). *Understanding state constitutions*. Princeton University Press.

*Tennessee County Government Handbook, County Technical Assistance Service*. (2010). The University of Tennessee.

Tolbert, C. J., Grummel, J. A., & Smith, D. A. (2001). The effects of ballot initiatives on voter turnout in the American states. *American Politics Research*, *29*(6), 625-648.

U.S. Const., amend. XXII.

U.S. Const., pmbl.

Vile, J. R., & Byrnes, M. E. (1998). *Tennessee government and politics: Democracy in the Volunteer State*. Vanderbilt University Press.

Wattenberg, M. P., McAllister, I., & Salvanto, A. (2000). How voting is like taking an SAT test: An analysis of American voter rolloff. *American Politics Quarterly*, *28*(2), 234-250.

Williams, N. R. (2006). Executive Review in the Fragmented Executive: State Constitutionalism and Same-Sex

Marriage. *University of Pennsylvania Law Review, 154*(3), 565-648.

Yager, J. (2010). GAO: Appointees given employment may not be most qualified. *The Hill.*

## ABOUT THE AUTHOR

David Lon Page holds a Doctorate of Philosophy in Electrical Engineering from the University of Tennessee and is a Research Scientist in computer vision. He is an amateur political junky and has been active in politics, volunteering in campaigns since the age of ten. He has also dreamed of being a professional flag football player, but those dreams have never materialized. However, he hopes the current plan to host flag football in the 2028 Los Angeles Olympics offers rekindled belief in his dream. As he awaits the Olympics to come calling, David pines and lives in Knoxville, Tennessee, with his wife, Lisa, and their daughter, Grace.

www.ingramcontent.com/pod-product-compliance
Lightning Source LLC
Chambersburg PA
CBHW070630030426
42337CB00020B/3972